Young Writers 2006 Creative Wi

small talk

In The Land Of Make-Believe
Vol I

Edited by Lynsey Hawkins

p172

Chloë Roper

2006

Disclaimer

Young Writers has maintained every effort
to publish stories that will not cause offence.

Any stories, events or activities relating to individuals
should be read as fictional pieces and not construed
as real-life character portrayal.

 Young**Writers**
First published in Great Britain in 2006 by:
Young Writers
Remus House
Coltsfoot Drive
Peterborough
PE2 9JX
Telephone: 01733 890066
Website: www.youngwriters.co.uk

SB ISBN 1 84602 679 2

Foreword

All children love to read and be read to, and what would delight a child more than writing their very own piece that others can read and have read to them?

Young Writers was established in 1991 to promote the written word amongst school children. Now, in 2006, we are still encouraging children to put themselves forward and to challenge their own talents, especially through specifically tailored projects such as our short story challenge promoted through primary schools nationwide.

To ensure the writer was challenged and that the books offer a variety of writing styles and themes we offered pupils the opportunity to write a short story on a theme of their choice. Alternatively they could have used one of the following to inspire their piece; *the Mini Saga*, a story of 50 words or less; the saga has a beginning, middle and end, often with a twist in the tale. *Nursery Rhymes & Fairy Tales* - we suggested the idea of pupils writing a letter to a character such as Fantasy Forest Council writing to the Big Bad Wolf. As well as that inspiration could be drawn from the theme to write a monologue, a spell, to re-tell a fairy tale, change the ending or even mix and match the characters in stories!

Each piece was chosen on the basis of style, technical skill, ability to entertain and flair for writing, and from the many entries we received, we have produced an outstanding 'Small Talk' series of books, with the pieces written by 7-11 year-olds, all illustrating how imaginative today's children can be. *Small Talk - In The Land Of Make-Believe Vol I* is our latest offering which we are sure you will agree is a fantastic collection, not only showcasing the pupils' work, but the school's ability to inspire and let the children's creativity flow.

We hope you continue to enjoy this delightful collection again and again for it is truly inspired and a credit to all who are featured within the following pages.

Contents

James Brocklehurst (11)   60
Demi-Leigh Astill (10)   61
Emma Savidge (11)   62
Louise Calvert (10)   63
Josh Kingsland (11)   64
Sharna Francis (11)   65
Josh Cook (10)   66
Amber Coles (8)   67
Alison Brown (11)   68
Taylor Buck   69
Jodi McQuade (9)   70

Gunthorpe CE Primary School, Nottingham

Catriona Sutcliffe (8)   71
Hugh Harland (9)   72
Ryan Wetton-Byrne (9)   73
Lydia Skerritt (9)   74
Joe Brownley (9)   75
Katy Southgate (9)   76
Jack Simms (9)   77
Charlotte Mayo (9)   78
Bethany Hampson-Smith (9)   79
Amy Keane (8)   80
Georgia Simpson (8)   81
Jemma Mills (9)   82
Amy Frogson (9)   83
Kelsi Lucas (8)   84
Courtney Abell (8)   85
Lewis Mayo (8)   86
Adam Deverill (9)   87
Callum Slack (8)   88
Catherine Angus (8)   89
Ava Stevens (7)   90
Jordan Slack (8)   91

Heathfield Primary School, Nottingham

Tyler Guy (10)   92
Antonio Palinczuk (10)   93
Hannah Musovic (10)   94
Rowan Sipson (10)   95

Katie Ridley (10)	96
Jade Unwin (11)	97

Henry Whipple Junior School, Nottingham

Aimen Arshad (11)	98
Jak Hamilton (10)	99
Shelby Kerry (11)	100
Kerry Bonser (11)	101
Rebekha Bedding (11)	102
George Tomlinson (11)	103
Adam Bellamy (11)	104
Mathew Whittaker (11)	105

Milbrook Primary School, Grove

Adam Lockwood (10)	106
Dominic Thackray (10)	107
Gaby Beckley (9)	108
Shane Harris (10)	109
Thomas Fell (10)	110
Maxwell Williams (10)	111
Abbie Ellis (10)	112
Deborah Martin (10)	113
George Audas (9)	114
Paige Watts (10)	115
Luke Kirkland (9)	116
Timothy Cloete (10)	117
Ian Cotton (10)	118
Luke Parsons (10)	119
Robyn Grundy (10)	120
Alex Frost (10)	121
Paige Aitken (10)	122
Gemma Tuckey (10)	123
Abbie Norton (10)	124
Amy Brazier (10)	125
Jake Griffin (10)	126
Pippa Peart (10)	127
Emily Smith (10)	128
Joshua Woodbridge (10)	129
Kieran Pope (10)	130
Jack Wellstood (10)	131
Jay Thomas (10)	132

Rebecca Warboys (9)   133
Joshua Patrick (10)   134
Rhiannon Hurst (10)   135
Alice Cox (9)   136
Maia Sprules (10)   137
Yasmin Bahar (10)   138
Tyler Curtis (9)   139
Sara Coakley (9)   140

Rampton Primary School, Retford

Josh Gillott (10)   141
Sarah Hinds (9)   142

Sonning Common Primary School, Reading

George Frank (10)   143
Matthew Outram (10)   144
Sophie Lewis (10)   145
Jacob Lee (11)   146
Robert Kenrick (11)   147
Amy Chadwick (10)   148
George Maxted (10)   149
Ben Sharpe (10)   150
Laura Burgess (10)   151

Wood's Foundation Primary School, Woodborough

Anna Snape   152
George Gamble (10)   153
Jacob Radford (10)   154
David Walker (10)   155
Jack Boaden (10)   156
Eleanor Sharkey (10)   157
Ryan Skeels (10)   158
Tamsin Smith (10)   159
Jane Fraser (9)   160
Katherine Driver (10)   161
Holly Smith (10)   162
Josie Perry (9)   163
Joe Desmond (10)   164
Jemma Lynch (10)   165
Elicia Cowley (10)   166
Rachel Martin (10)   167

The Creative Writing

Dark Forest

There once was a 12-year-old girl called Sarah. She had a sister called Lucy, who was 3 and two brothers called Jack, 9, and Sam, 7. Their parents were away on holiday in Spain. They lived in a cottage beside a dark forest and their parents said not to go into it. Lucy and Sam were afraid of the dark forest.

One foggy day Sam was out playing tennis with Jack. Sam had the ball and he gave it one *big* shot and it went far into the forest. Sam forgot that his mum had warned him not to go in, so Sam went to look for it. Jack kept shouting, 'Come back, come back!' but Sam didn't listen. Jack ran in and told Sarah what had happened. Sarah was too scared to ring her mum because she was scared what her mum would do.

Sam walked through the forest looking for the ball. Just then he saw it. He ran and picked it up. 'Yes,' he shouted. He didn't know the way home, but he turned around and he saw a window of the house. He ran and he ran and he got to the house. Sarah, Jack and Lucy came running out.

'Are you alright?' worried Sarah.

'Yes, I'm fine,' said Sam.

Mum and Dad rang home and said they were coming home. All the rooms were a bit of a mess so they quickly cleaned up the house.

After about two hours they arrived. They came into the house and asked if everything was alright.

'Yes,' they all said and they never told their mother and father about their adventure.

Rebecca Graham
Belleek Primary School, Enniskillen

Computer Capture

'This is *stupid!*' Maizy fumed. 'Mr Bopling said my boring homework has to be in tomorrow, this rip-off computer will not work!' Banging her fist on the machine, she walked out the room.

Her dad walked in, exclaiming, 'Well, don't say I never do anything for you Maze, I found a computer mechanic, he's coming at 6.30!'

Maizy smiled, 'Thanks Dad, but I don't think it will work, the stupid machine's all burned out, it was smoking yesterday.'

They laughed. Her dad continued, 'He's coming anyway.'

He came and went to Maizy's room, fiddled with her computer, then came downstairs and told everyone it was fixed. He was paid and gone in a flash. 'He was quick,' Maizy said. After watching TV, she went to bed.

It was about 3 o'clock. Suddenly Maizy's computer started bleeping. Maizy woke to banging, then before she could scream, the screen bubbled. Maizy started being sucked into the computer. She was captured.

Maizy looked around. All she saw was digits. Suddenly a huge number 9 was in front of her, she gasped as she felt herself being sucked into the digit. 'Help,' she screamed, but no one heard.

Now when she looked around she saw people. But they were computer game style. She looked up and saw the mechanic. 'Where am I you creep?'

'In my game, you'll stay forever!' he hushed, smiling. 'Bye-bye.' Then everything went dark.

'What's happening?' Maizy whispered.

'He's turned us off,' someone said.

'How can we get out?'

'We can't.'

Eleni Gospel (11)
Broomhill Junior School, Nottingham

The Surprise Birthday Party For Beth

One day a little girl called Beth realised that her birthday was in two days. She said to her mum, 'Can I have a birthday party please?'

'No.'

'Please!'

'No and that's final!'

Beth stormed up to her room, rang her best friends Katie, Haylie and Dayna. They all felt sorry for her.

The next morning Chloe, her mum, went up to Beth's room and said, 'Your dad can't take you to school today, so I will have to take you instead.'

'Whatever.'

'Don't talk to me like that!' shouted her mum. Her mum went down the stairs and Beth followed. 'Where's your bobble, Beth?'

'I don't know,' Beth replied.

'You're going to have to wear a pink one.'

'Whatever!'

Whilst Chloe, her mum, was doing her hair she just screamed for no reason. 'Why did you scream?'

'Because you pulled my hair!'

'No I didn't!'

Beth was half an hour late.

All day parents were helping set the surprise birthday party for when Beth arrived home. Beth was the last one out of school. When she arrived home the lights were out so Beth turned them on and everyone shouted, *'Surprise!'*

Beth ran up to her mum and said, 'Thank you.' Chloe gave her the present that she'd bought her and it was a kitten. Beth called it Spot and Chloe, Beth, her dad and Spot, lived happily ever after!

Chloe Newcombe (8)
Broomhill Junior School, Nottingham

When Broghan Came To Sleep At The Bungalow

It was Wednesday and Broghan came to sleep. Then the electricity went off and I walked into the bookshelf and knocked all the books off. Just then Broghan walked in the door and we just laughed. Then she said she needed the toilet. My dad came in with a pretend bat and started hitting us with it and we shouted, 'Stop it.' It was quite soft. He apologised and we went to bed.

On Thursday we told our friends and they giggled all day. At home time we had to say goodbye and our friends told our mums the story and they were laughing too.

On Friday my dad talked to Lisa all about the evening. She laughed and we all joined in.

On Saturday she came round for a few hours and we watched the television and we had a power cut and we all shouted, 'Oh no ...' and we started laughing.

Emily Plaskitt (8)
Broomhill Junior School, Nottingham

Untitled

The burglar stared into the house, it was deserted. He crept inside and saw lots of jewels. Something caught his attention. He put it in his bag, it began to glow.

Suddenly his bag began to swell and swell and swell. It started to suffocate him.

Michael Allinson (10)
Broomhill Junior School, Nottingham

Fear!

My hands were shaking and I was nearly sick. My mouth vibrated more each second.

Suddenly we zoomed downwards. I screamed. When we landed on the ground I wished that I wasn't so scared about riding on roller coasters.

Lucy Kennedy (9)
Broomhill Junior School, Nottingham

Goldilocks And The Three Hairs

One day, Goldilocks was hungry and tired. She found a little small head in the middle of the forest. 'I think I will go inside and see what's in there,' said Goldilocks.

'Argh!' Goldilocks ran away and the three hairs chased after her. Down the forest, up the hill and underground.

Then they went into the three bears' house.

'Hey,' said Mother Bear, 'this is our story, not yours!'

Toby Michael (8)
Burton Joyce Primary School, Nottingham

Jack And The Junjerbrad Man

(For Pete's sake, he's a baby, how would he know how to spell Gingerbread!)

One day, Jack felt like making a cake, so he made junjerbrad. *Breep, breep!* 'He's burnt!' screeched Jack.

The junjerbrad man started to run. Jack said, 'Run little Junjer, run.'

Junjer got to a river.

A fox said, 'Do ...'

'No thanks, I've got my five metres badge,' said Junjer.

'Sorry,' said the fox.

'That's OK.'

Henry Smith (9)
Burton Joyce Primary School, Nottingham

Goldifox And The Three Pears

Once upon a time there was a fox called Goldifox. He went through the forest and he found a cottage. He went inside and found three bowls of Weetabix but the milk had gone off.

Then Goldifox found three sofas but ... the first was far too hard. The second was too high and the last was just right and he fell asleep.

Then the pears came back and found ... Goldifox. Then he woke up and ate Baby Pear.

'Argh!'

Eloise Pindor (8)
Burton Joyce Primary School, Nottingham

Goldifox And The Blue Bears

One day in May, Goldifox was sprinting through the forest. Suddenly he came across a small mouse. He went inside the mouse, it had big furniture.

He explored inside the mouse. All the things inside the mouse were blue and big. He came across some blue porridge. He tried the porridge. Blue Baddy Bear's was too cold, Brother Bear's was too hot and Baby Bear's was just right, so he ate it all up. Next he tried the pears. Baby Bear's was too small. Brother Bear's too big and Baddy Bear's was OK. After that he tried the heads. Baby Bear's was too tall, Baddy Bear's was too low and Brother Bear's was OK. He went downstairs and covered the floor in blue glue. Goldifox went back to head.

The three blue bears were back. 'Oh no,' all the bears shouted. They had got stuck. Goldifox used them as statues. After all blue was his favourite colour.

Layla Hallam-Huggins (9)
Burton Joyce Primary School, Nottingham

Goldisocks And The Three Chairs

Once upon a time, there were three chairs. Their names were Big Poppa Chair, Middle-Sized Chair and Baby Chair. One day a girl named Goldisocks was walking through the woods when she saw the three chairs walking out of a door. The fast one didn't close the door, so when the three chairs had gone out of sight she went inside and looked around.

She was still looking around when she saw some solid porridge. She tried the first bowl of porridge. 'Too cold.' Then she tried the second bowl of porridge. 'Too hot.' Then there was only the fast bowl left so she tried the fast bowl of porridge, but she had to catch it first. 'Lovely,' and she ate it all up.

Then she came to some bears. She looked at them all and said, 'They look very comfortable, I'll try them out. So she sat on the first bear. 'Way too hard.' Then she tried the second bear. 'Way too soft.' She tried the fast bear. It stayed still this time, so she sat down on the fast bear but she was a but too heavy and *crash,* the setting fell down right on top of Goldisocks.

Georgina Durkin (8)
Burton Joyce Primary School, Nottingham

The Ugly Duckling

There was once a beautiful duckling called The Ugly. He lived with his mum, dad and little brother. His brother was always picking on him because everyone else was ugly. But even though they were all ugly, he liked being beautiful.

Years past without him looking in the mirror. (Since that was when he got picked on.) But he missed the mirror so he looked in it and … *he was ugly* and his brother was beautiful, so he started to cry.

Megan Crawley (9)
Burton Joyce Primary School, Nottingham

Goldilocks And The Three Sets Of Stairs

One day, there was a girl named Goldilocks. She looked through a window and saw three sets of stairs. She opened the door and walked in. She wanted to go upstairs.

The first set of stairs was too steep. The second set was still too steep, but the third set was just right!

I would carry on writing the story, but my favourite programme is on, so … not the end …

Joshua Blackwell (8)
Burton Joyce Primary School, Nottingham

Golden Socks And The Three Hairs!

One May day the three hairs had a bowl of head lice to eat, but the lice were too hot so the hairs decided to have a talk in the wood. When they were out a pair of socks that were the colour gold appeared out of nowhere!

The socks went into the house and tried and tried and tried to eat the lice but it couldn't because 1) the socks didn't have a mouth and 2) the lice ran away.

So then the socks sat on the hairs' chair but the chair didn't break. 'Hooray,' shouted one of the golden socks. The socks went to the red bed and they slept there for a 1,000 years. I can't be bothered to write any more so this is ... the end!

Hannah Cluff (9)
Burton Joyce Primary School, Nottingham

Viking At War

My face was dripping in sweat and my feet firmly on the ground. With my axe in one hand and a shield in the other, we charged violently at the enemy.

The roars and helpless cries could be heard by the gods above. The war was over, we had won.

Andrew Davis (11)
Charley Memorial Primary School, Belfast

Ghost

Once there were two ghosts. They went to a house. It was called Ghost Manor and a person called Jenny came to the house and changed it into a real house and had a party.

It was wonderful. However, the ghosts haunted her all year. But the ghosts stopped suddenly …

Charlie McGreevey (9)
Charley Memorial Primary School, Belfast

The Attic

Crash! I looked around. Nothing there. *Crash!* Another box had fallen. *Fixt* … no lights. Then the trapdoor closed. I was left alone.

'Help me,' I screamed. Suddenly the lights buzzed on and the door swung open. I ran downstairs, My mum told me that it was just a power cut. *Phew!*

Anne Henderson (9)
Charley Memorial Primary School, Belfast

My Dog Tia

I went to the dog pound. I was scared, I gripped my mum's hand tightly. When I got in I saw a little puppy. She was so cute. I asked my mum if we could get her and we did. We brought her home the next day. Tia's her name.

Emma Thompson (11)
Charley Memorial Primary School, Belfast

Bedtime Saga

'I want to leave,' I shouted.

My mum came running in, 'What's the matter?' she asked.

'Nothing,' I replied sleepily.

My mum went back to bed and I fell asleep again.

'I want to leave now!' I shouted again.

My dad came in. 'It's only a dream,' I told him.

Ami Thompson (11)
Charley Memorial Primary School, Belfast

The Noise

I heard something, I stopped. The floor started to move. Oh no, I fell over wondering what was happening. Then my sister came down and said, 'What's wrong?'

I didn't know. The floor stopped moving then started again. I looked outside, there was a big tractor outside in the field.

Kimberley Johnston (9)
Charlton Primary School, Wantage

Weird Stuff

I saw a massive door. I went through. *Suddenly,* there was a monster. A big hairy monster. My heart was pounding so I tried to fight it viciously.

But, *'Argh!'* I went through a tiny trapdoor. Then I was in my room, snuggled in my bed. What a night!

Andrew Hurst (8)
Charlton Primary School, Wantage

Daydreaming

Wheeeeee. *Bang!* Ouch, my head hit the sides. Over to one side then over to the other. 'Argh!'

Crash! The Tardis had landed. I was in bed, my bed.

I went into a kitchen, my mum was there, oh it was just a silly dream.

Jemma Jaques (9)
Charlton Primary School, Wantage

A Letter To Pied Piper

Dear Pied Piper,

Why did you take the children into that dark, spooky cave? They may have been scared. Were you scared of those incy-wincy mice?

I must say you are a good pipe player. Well I hope you never come to Wantage, where I live. I don't want mice crawling under my feet or you taking me into a cave.

Yours hopefully

Jana.

PS And don't get my friends either.

Jana Cooper (9)
Charlton Primary School, Wantage

I Hate My New House

I was in the car and the car was moving. I waved goodbye to my warming old house and blew a tiny kiss at it. I clutched my teddy and all my friends' addresses. I was leaving and there was nothing I could do about it. I stared out of the window and sighed. I wish I didn't have to move house.

My heart sank as I saw my new house, it was so boring, all the red brick walls and spiky hedges. I ran upstairs to see my room, my mum had said it was really big. When I saw it my heart sank even deeper it felt like it was so deep it was in my toes. Yes, it was bigger but not better, it had a golden carpet with matching walls and curtains. The bed was enormous and had lots of tiny pillows. It was horrid.

My dad walked in with a huge box of new clothes. Oh no, I hate it. My dad was not the kind of person you would like to talk to, in fact sometimes I think he doesn't even know how to speak. My mum was the total opposite, she knows how to speak alright. She can't stop talking.

Suddenly, I heard a crash downstairs. It was the painting and it had been smashed and behind the painting was a cracked wall. So maybe we might be moving back after all.

Poppy Deacon (9)
Charlton Primary School, Wantage

The Desert

One hot day in the desert, explorer Sam Grimes and his noble trusted friend Adam Tomson were searching eagerly for treasure. Sam and Adam looked fruitlessly for the treasure. Just then Sam fell into a hole. Adam shouted down, 'Are you OK?' There was no reply. Little did Adam know Sam had run down a mysterious passageway.

Something from the jet-black darkness groaned, 'Oh!'

'Argh!' screamed Sam. He began to walk forward when *roar.* Sam ran right back as speedy as he could through the passageway, he just managed to climb out. Adam saw the monster that made the noises. It was horrible and totally terrifying. It had piercing red eyes and really sharp teeth.

They both ran for their lives. They were in hot pursuit by the monster when *bang!* The monster had tripped over the pyramid. Sam woke up. 'Phew, it was just a dream.'

Henry McColl (9)
Charlton Primary School, Wantage

The Roller Coaster

My head was spinning, my hands were sweating and I just felt sick. I wanted to get off but I knew I couldn't. We went up and up and up, we were about to go off the edge. I shut my eyes as tight as I could. We went off the edge. I screamed.

Seconds later, as I stepped onto non-moving land, I said to myself, 'Next time I am not going in the mini Teletubbie ride!'

Catherine Arnott (9)
Charlton Primary School, Wantage

Rumbling Aeroplane

The tremendous rumble started. I bounced and shuddered on my seat. It got worse. *Shatter, shatter, bounce, bounce!* My ears shrieked like I was in a tug-of-war. It stopped on the aeroplane.

Tom Walker (8)
Charlton Primary School, Wantage

The Haunted House

One blustery night I was fast asleep dreaming in my bed but not just a dream … a nightmare.

It all started when I was walking back from school and suddenly I found a house with broken windows with a blocked door. Anyway, I climbed through a broken window and saw someone lying on the floor. But then … 'Argh!'

Mum and Dad came running in saying, 'Wake up, wake up.'

I woke up with Dad saying, 'It was only a dream!'

Rebecca Bolton (9)
Charlton Primary School, Wantage

Dragon Football

Football, a lively game about a ball, a foot, a goal and players! Some people think football's just for boys, think again.

Holly was just 6 years old when she started playing football for Firewell Dragons under 12s. Now she's 11, she plays brilliantly and being captain of her team makes her quite popular.

The only thing is she gets very nervous when she plays in a big match and today a match was about to start.

'OK, Firewell, high knees, high knees,' their coach Mr Rowen chanted at the team.

Puff, puff went the Dragons onto the pitch.

'I'm really nervous,' Holly said to Ziggy, her best friend.

As the other team appeared on the pitch Firewell got into their positions and got ready for the kick-off.

3, 2, 1, bang! The ball went flying through the air at Johnny Plow's kick. The crowd went silent. Straight into the … goal! Everyone screamed as the scoreboards clicked Firewell 1 Blowin 0.

When everyone calmed down the game continued.

'Johnny to Ziggy. Ziggy missed. Sarah from Blowin, has the ball heading towards the goal. *Shoot!* No, Blowin have scored. There was a cheer from the Blowins followed by a gasp as the goalkeeper from Firewell was hit by the ball. It was time for a new goalkeeper to be sent on.

It was the last five minutes as Matthew the goalkeeper got into his position. The game had begun. Suddenly a huge kick and Firewell scored …

Anna Hurst (10)
Charlton Primary School, Wantage

The Magic Phonebook

(Story based on idea and childhood game played with friend Kate Farrelly (10)
Charlton Primary School)

Hi, I'm called Alexa and here's my story. I was walking along the road with my two friends called Ruby and Rob. Suddenly we came across an old house. We went up to it and Rob knocked on the door. Surprisingly the door was open. We went inside but Ruby whispered, 'We shouldn't go in anyone's house without permission.' We just ignored her and went on inside. Ruby followed on after a few seconds.

We went upstairs to have a look around. I opened a wardrobe and a book fell out. It said the words: *Magic Phonebook.* I had a look through it and it said all these places like haunted mansion and I called Ruby and Rob. I said, 'Let's go somewhere.'

Ruby and Rob agreed, so we all put our hands on the haunted mansion and we were there in a flash.

Suddenly a ghost came running after us. We hid in a wardrobe and I checked to see if anyone was out there, there wasn't so we got out and we started to walk down the hall. I heard a noise, I looked behind me and I screamed, it was a vampire. So I shouted, 'Run!'

We ran so fast that the vampire was out of sight. I said, 'Let's get out of here.'

They both agreed so we put our hands on the picture and we were back at last. So we got out the house and went home, I held tight to the magic phonebook.

Sarah Perry (9)
Charlton Primary School, Wantage

The Mole Hole

Far, far away lived a huge group of happy moles on a huge hill. The whole mound of grass was covered in holes, some big, some small, all dotted around. All these combination of holes were made for the different sizes of the moles who were living in them.

This is a story of one of these moles who was very dim. He was one of the big ones. His name was Harry.

One day when Harry had just had a good meal with his jolly friend Bart he was just going to his hole (well to what he thought it was) when he wished he wasn't so fat.

He jumped into his hole then suddenly he stopped. He was stuck. He had gone in the wrong hole! He wiggled and jiggled and pushed as much as he could but his tummy wouldn't move.

The next day he was still stuck, his friends had tried all night to pull him out. The king of moles told everyone to have a meeting where Harry was stuck. The meeting went on for quite a while until they came up with a brilliant idea. When Harry woke up from a little snooze in his uncomfortable position, he saw that he was in a huge hole, the moles had dug it all for themselves. They all were having the time of their lives and were all very pleased.

Jennifer Culshaw (10)
Charlton Primary School, Wantage

War Of The Beast

Whack! Whack! Argh!

The next thing I knew it was 3.27, around two hours after the fight. I was going to crush him, one way or another. I picked myself up, then I heard a voice, 'I will crush you personally.'

And he did, so here I am dead.

In my new world there is a war on getting revenge on deaths of the beast. The Revenge Rebellion KTBFFAMFAR (kill the beast for freedom and more freedom and revenge). So here I am on the blazing front line getting torn apart by the beast. So remember whenever you see the beast, *kill him!*

Calum Thomson (9)
Charlton Primary School, Wantage

Dear Three Bears

Dear Three Bears,

Why, why, why? How could you send me out of your house: I know, I know, maybe I did bring mud in from the pigsty, but it's not my fault, you don't even have a doormat.

OK, OK, I did eat your porridge, but I was so hungry I hadn't had any breakfast because I wasn't allowed after dialling 999 on my dad's phone. I dialled 999 on my dad's phone because it was upside down, I didn't know and 666 is my best friend's phone number. I wanted her to come and play. Anyway, yes I went in your bed but I was so tired after falling off a horse and stinging myself on a bumblebee.

Do you have no heart?

Yours from, who you think is a criminal, but is really an angel.

Goldilocks.

Greta Piras (8)
Charlton Primary School, Wantage

A Letter To Baby Bear

Dear Baby Bear,

I am so sorry I ate all your porridge and broke your chair. Your bed felt so warm and snugly that I just went off to sleep. My mother was very cross when I told her about what I had done, she was mad at me but she told me that she would give you a whole sack of porridge and my dad said he would make you a new chair and I'm going to do my bit too and invite you to my party.

It will be 2-3pm on the 21st July. We will play party games and have a delicious tea and guess what … I'm going to be 6 years old. It seems ages since I was born. Hope you can come. Please wear a pink dress!

From Goldilocks.

PS I didn't do all those things you think I did. It was my puppy Digit. And it was my parrot, Stripes, who flew into the window and broke the glass. I called him Stripes because he doesn't have stripes. I didn't do all those things even though you think I did. I'm a little angel, honest. See ya. GL.

Alice Ferguson (8)
Charlton Primary School, Wantage

The Monster

My heart missed a beat. I trembled. The creaks got louder. I could feel a lump coming in my throat. I imagined all different kinds of monsters.

Suddenly my cat Smudge jumped on my bed. *Phew*, I wish I didn't have such a fear of being alone.

Sophie Liquorish (9)
Charlton Primary School, Wantage

Snow White In Norway

In a town not so far away, lived a young girl called Snow White. Her long blonde hair was tied up, keeping it out of the bright red paint. Dabbing at the clay trolls her dad had cast that morning, she was thinking about her dead mother.

As she painted, her dad approached and whispered, 'I am getting remarried.' The expression on Snow White's face was one of anger and excitement combined.

The wedding day arrived. A bony white figure glided down the aisle towards Snow White's dad. The vows were exchanged. The deed was done. Snow White's heart sank.

The stepmother was envious of Snow White's beautiful sea craft. She plotted to kill her, ordering her to be thrown off a cliff. But she was left cold and alone as her assassin could not do it. Luckily, seven fishermen were sailing past and took pity on her. 'Can you fish?'

The next day Snow White had caught the biggest fish in town. Everyone knew about it including the evil stepmother! This was going to spoil her party. No one noticed her slip the poison into Snow White's seafood. The party began … and Snow White ended.

Bearing the coffin, came the seven fishermen. Slipping on the mossy path, one of them dropped the shining box. Out shot the poisoned shrimp and Snow White opened her eyes. Looking up, Snow White noticed a young skier speeding down the mountains. It was love at first sight!

Harry Stockwell (11)
Crossdale Drive Primary School, Nottingham

Little Red Roller Skates

Once upon a time there lived a girl named Little Red Roller Skates. Little Red's mother asked her to visit her grandmother at the retirement home. So Little Red reluctantly rolled on her way.

When she arrived at grandma's home, the door triggered a bell at the reception desk and a blonde woman came out of the staffroom. 'How can I help?' asked the woman cautiously.

'I'm visiting Shirley Skates,' she said.

'Room 47,' replied the woman, already walking away.

Little Red finally reached '47' and knocked. No answer. Grandma had a thing for personal security, so why was the door ajar? Cautiously she slid through the gap. A figure by the window spun round.

'What a bald head you have Grandma! Is it your new pills?' asked Red Roller Skates.

'Urr,' said the person. A man it seemed. Little Red Roller Skates looked him up and down.

'Where's Grandma? Why have you got her things?' she shouted. She dashed towards the man and gave him a sly rabbit-punch to the forehead. He was out cold in a second. Effortlessly she dragged him out the room. 'Grandma? Where are you?' she called.

Loud bangs came from inside the wardrobe. 'Red Roller Skates,' Grandma croaked, tears rolling down her cheeks. After hugging her, Little Red helped Grandma out. They celebrated until six.

'I'm going now Grandma.'

'Alright, come again soon.'

'I will Grandma,' said Red Roller Skates … but she had her fingers crossed behind her back.

Bethany Jenkins (11)
Crossdale Drive Primary School, Nottingham

In The Bath

I am lying here in the pool, I've forgotten to put my armbands on. I see the lifeguard coming, I scream. 'Argh!' Suddenly I remember I am only in the bath and my brother's pulled out the plug so the water isn't there. *Gurgle, gurgle, gurgle!*

Rebecca Roberts (11)
Derriaghy Primary School, Lisburn

The Winning Goal

My legs are shaking, the sweat is dripping down my face, I don't know what to do. I look around me and people are screaming, people are getting closer. I look up and down and kick the ball. I score!

Lauren Hanna (11)
Derriaghy Primary School, Lisburn

Singing For The 'X Factor'

As I walk onto the stage my legs shake, then I hear the crowd screaming and whistling. I get so nervous I stand in the middle of the stage then look at the judges. The music starts and my voice trembles, then Simon Cowell tells me to stop. 'You're through!'

Chantelle Woods (11)
Derriaghy Primary School, Lisburn

Simpsons Hit And Run

I'm driving along in the car at 80mph on the motorway. I'm overtaking all the cars. I'm coming to a red light, but there is no way I'm stopping. So I drive right through it. Nooooo! All of a sudden I crash.

Then my X-Box goes off.

Nicole Smyth (10)
Derriaghy Primary School, Lisburn

Match Of The Day

Liverpool vs Manchester United.

Kick-off, Ronaldo is on the ball he's tackled by Crouch and passes it to Rooney. Rooney shoots, *goal!* The score is 1-0 at half-time.

Liverpool kick-off, Cisse and Crouch kick-off, Cisse is at the goalkeeper's box. Cisse shoots, the keeper saves it. Whistle blows.

Ross Bassett (10)
Derriaghy Primary School, Lisburn

The Butterfingers Club

There was a caveman called Tom. He had a club to hit people with, he called it Martha. Martha and Tom loved each other, they had so much fun beating people up.

One day Tom was about to hit a cobra with Martha, but then a pterodactyl snatched Martha out of Tom's greasy butterfingers. He licked the butter off his fingers and then called out to Martha. Martha didn't hear and loved the ride. The pterodactyl flew the whole way up to George the volcano and set Martha in its nest before flying off.

Tom decided to ride on his pet giant bullfrog Pete, to get to Martha. The volcano was starting to erupt. 'Duh … volcano got bellyache,' called Tom. He got to the volcano, got off Pete and started climbing. He climbed and climbed until the writer got a cramp. He finally got to the nest and grabbed Martha.

'Me save you … uh … Martha!' cried Tom.

'Look out!' cried Martha as the lava from the volcano came closer.

He saw the pterodactyl fly over. Tom grabbed onto it and it flew them away. 'Phew … this never would have happened if you weren't such a butterfingers Tom,' said Martha.

'Sorry … but … me like butter,' said Tom and they went back to squashing the cobra.

Robyn Kelly (11)
Doagh Primary School, Doagh

Murder

We were walking down the street when 10 teenagers jumped out of nowhere. We ran but they were faster. They stabbed Jack but I got away. I ran down an alleyway. They stabbed my leg but I survived. I limped to hospital and called the police but they never caught the gang.

Later that year outside my house kids were shouting racist comments at me. At night they were arrested. When I was 20 I lost my job, we were robbed. Mum's car was stolen. When I walk down the street I hear rude comments. Is it because I'm black?

Zeph Catachanas Rossin (10)
Dunkirk Primary School, Nottingham

My Diary

I don't feel happy in this country. It makes me feel like I don't fit in. Every day when I walk to school I see the gang of bullies that always pick on me. But whenever the teachers are watching they always act nicely. I'm afraid that if I tell on them they will do more damage. I always have to sit by myself at lunchtime because I have no friends. I am the only black person in the school, even the teachers are white. It's a Christian school and we don't even talk about black culture or people, only when we talk about how the English made them become part of their empire.

So really I have nobody to stick up for me. Most people even say that the head teacher was forced to take me and only took me to make her look like someone who understands how it feels to be someone that is different and no one likes. It makes me feel like no one in the world cares about me and other people of different colour. Especially when they say things like they said about the head teacher.

Sometimes I wish that I lived somewhere nice. This place comes into my dreams too. It's somewhere no one gets bullied and there are no bullies anyway. Also in this fantasy land are lovely people and delicious fruit, vegetables and food. When I woke up I know I've been dreaming.

Eshe Graham (10)
Dunkirk Primary School, Nottingham

Dear Diary

Dear Diary,

I'm moving house soon and I'm going to a new school. I'm so happy I'm moving, nobody in my school likes me for two reasons. First of all because I come from Pakistan, secondly because of what I did.

I'll tell you, there was a girl from Africa called Maya who was always mean to me and one day she was so mean to me that I just burst. I called her so many names that I had thought about at home, but I never thought that I would call Maya these names but I did. I didn't mean to they just slipped out. I got really told off and nobody wanted to be my friend anymore.

Dear Diary,

We moved yesterday, our new house is lovely and cosy and I visited my new school and it looks good. I'm going to be in class 6A, my teacher is going to be Mrs Pefuntia, she is an odd lady, she has bright red curly hair and has a high-pitched voice. I love my new room, I painted it blue with purple stripes. I got a new bunk bed and tomorrow I'm going to get a puppy.

Dear Diary,

I started my new school today, I'm not sure who likes me though. Nobody wanted to be my partner in PE, this girl called Scarlet called me a … I'm not going to tell you what she called me. I hope she won't do it again. Anyway, I have a new puppy he is so cute I called him Zulo.

Dear Diary,

Scarlet calls me every day now. She's been doing it for 3 weeks! In front of the teachers she's a goody-two-shoes but in the playground she torments me. I hate her but this time I did the right thing, I told someone.

Fiona Garrahan (10)
Dunkirk Primary School, Nottingham

The Three Billy Goats Gruff

Dear Diary,

Today I can't believe I'm still alive! After those dumb, greedy animals invaded my home. I should have eaten the smallest and medium goats. Here's what happened: I was sleeping after a long night of fishing, but then heard footsteps. I got up there as fast as I could and saw the first glance of what was up there. I let the first one go because he was a pip-squeak. Then I heard some more footsteps and clambered up again, but the other goat was still small. Then the grand daddy of all came up. He was the fattest. I blocked the way past me and I was going for the throat but then … *bang!* He knocked me flying around the moon twice (which was pretty amazing) then crashed into the water. Quickly I swam towards an underwater cavern. That's where I am now and the only thing I'm eating is crabs, oysters and fish. *Curse you goats!*

Benjamin Luck (9)
Glapton Primary & Nursery School, Nottingham

The Three Billy Goats Gruff

Dear Diary,

What a day I have had today. I was woken and found that I was invaded. In fact, I'll tell you the whole story.

It all started at 3pm. I had just finished my fishing and caught nothing. Then all of a sudden, *trip-trap, trip-trap.* I felt as angry as a T-rex, nothing was going to stop me now. 'Who is that trip-trapping over my bridge?'

'It is only me the little Billy Goat Gruff,' he said squeakily.

I said, 'So what, I'm still going to eat you.'

'Eat the next goat, he's as fat as a bear.'

I said, 'OK.'

Then the next goat came, he looked tasty, but I let him go because he said the next one was as fat as a whale. *Yum-yum.* I went for him but he lowered his head and *bang* … I was lucky to have survived from Earth to Saturn. I am now living once again in the yucky old river.

Joe Cook (9)
Glapton Primary & Nursery School, Nottingham

Rhyming Red Riding Hood

One day, long ago in a house made of wood
A mother was lying in bed.
Her daughter Red Riding Hood
Threw back the duvet and said,
'Rise and shine, it's a new day,
Lots of work, lots of play.'
'I don't feel well,' Mother said,
'I must stay comfortable in my bed.
But take these delicious apple pies
They'll keep the tears out of Gran's eyes.'
So Red Riding Hood set off on her task
With some orange juice in a flask.
Meanwhile, a fierce wolf was hiding.
As he saw a girl called Red Riding
He ran to Gran's and hid inside.
Gran was dreaming of a fairground ride.
As soon as Red Riding Hood came to the house,
The wolf jumped out silent as a mouse.
'Yum, she looks delicious,' he said.
'Soon she will be dead.'
Gran woke up and hit the beast
And they were ready to roast him for their feast.
The wolf was never seen again
And that is the happy end!

Emma Barnett (9)
Glapton Primary & Nursery School, Nottingham

Rhyme Of Red Riding Hood

Little Red Riding Hood was as good as gold
But she wasn't very old.
Her mother was baking a pie that Little Red Riding Hood could smell.
Her mother said, 'Take this to your gran's because she's not

feeling well.'

She skipped along in her red riding hood
Through the deep dark wood.
A hungry wolf was nearby.
He was looking at her with his beady eye.
The wolf was racing through the trees
With his wibbly-wobbly knees.
Little Red Riding Hood was nearly there,
But the bad wolf was there and put Gran's clothes on
And put her in the bin.
Here comes Little Red Riding Hood skipping along.
She knocked on the door and the wolf said, 'Come in.'
So Little Red Riding Hood went in and into Gran's bedroom.
'What hairy hands you have Gran,' said Red Riding Hood,
'And what sharp teeth you have.'
She had a shotgun in a basket behind her back.
Then she shot the *big bad wolf.*
Nobody will ever be seeing the wolf again, so that's the end.

Sophie Phillipson (8)
Glapton Primary & Nursery School, Nottingham

The Three Billy Goats Gruff

The toughest of the tough
Belonged to the Three Billy Goats Gruff.
They had a certain problem which has never been solved.
I think it's best if we don't get involved.
So here comes the grizzly bit,
So let's not make too much of it.
He was ready to pounce
And further announce
What he was going to do
Was not actually quite true.
He was going to eat them up
For his brekkie, lunch and sup
When *big* Billy Goat Gruff came
Mr Troll came to harm and pain.
As he charged up he made the troll fly
60 miles high in the sky.

Demi Broughton (9)
Glapton Primary & Nursery School, Nottingham

Rhyme Of Red Riding Hood

One day there was a house and there, a little girl called Red Riding Hood lived. One day her grandma was poorly so she put some food in a basket and she had to walk through the woods. On the way she thought that she was being followed. A wolf was following her, the wolf had got to Grandma's house before Red Riding Hood. He put Grandma in the bin and dressed up like Grandma. Suddenly there was a knock on the door, 'Red Riding Hood, come on in,' the wolf said. So Red Riding Hood went in.

The wolf said to Red Riding Hood, 'Sit by my side, I'm going to eat you …'

James Huthwaite (8)
Glapton Primary & Nursery School, Nottingham

The Rhyme Of Little Red Riding Hood

One day there was a little girl whose hair was gold. Her mother was baking a pie. Little Red Riding Hood's mum asked her if she could take the pie to her grandmother. But Little Red Riding Hood was only six years old. The pie had a really nice smell. But before she left her mum said, 'Your granny isn't well.'

When she left she put up her hood. Carefully she walked through the wood. When she got halfway she heard a noise, she didn't know what it could be. It was a wolf, the wolf thought she looked tasty.

The wolf ran through the trees. He slipped and landed on his knees. Then got up and he still beat Little Red Riding Hood. He knocked on Grandma's door, she let him in. When she let him in he put her in a wheely bin. When Little Red Riding Hood arrived the wolf was in Grandma's disguise. The wolf shouted, 'Come in darling.'

She got the pie and threw it at him. The wolf cried out, 'I want my mummy.'

That was the end of the wolf. Little Red Riding Hood thought it was very funny.

Kayleigh Mitchell (9)
Glapton Primary & Nursery School, Nottingham

Untitled

There once was a girl called Red Riding Hood -
who had to go to her Gran who lived in the woods.
In her basket she took some very old books,
the rest she did not dare look.
So off she went to the busy bees' bush
and then she heard a terrifying crush.
When she got to Gran's she heard strange noises in the bin.
She just ignored it and went straight in.
She saw a different Gran in bed.
So this is what Red Riding Hood said,
'Why Gran, what big teeth you have.'
'The better to eat you with.'
When Gran got out of the dusty bin
the wolf got out, not daring to stay in.

Lily Ford
Glapton Primary & Nursery School, Nottingham

The Three Billy Goats Gruff

Dear Diary,

Today has been an exciting and terrifying day. It started when me, Little Billy Goat and of course Medium Billy Goat, had the most horrible day in history. It started here on a rocky hill called Goatsville. All the goats were enjoying themselves except me, Little Goat and Medium Goat, we were bored! We wanted something more than hard, crunchy waste and wanted to go to the meadow and eat soft, not crunchy, smooth, not hard, grass. 'We need something more,' I said in a small quiet voice. Cautiously we all looked over the bridge so I said, 'That's it, I can't stand it anymore. I'm going over that bridge and not coming back.' I plodded along the bridge, *clip-clop, clip-clop.*

'*Who is that on my bridge?*'

'It's only me,' I replied.

'Let me look, OK you can go you little nerd, go on.'

So Medium Billy Goat went over, *clip-clop, clip-clop.*

'*Who is that on my bridge?*'

'It is me,' said Medium Goat.

'Let me see you. OK, you may proceed, you smelly creature.'

'Now it's my turn. Here I come.' *Clip-clop, clip-clop.*

'*Who is that on my bridge?*'

'It is me the one, the only Big Billy Goat Gruff.'

'Let me see, now you are big and juicy, so I am going to eat you.'

'Oh no you're not.'

He lowered his horns and knocked the troll into the deep water. *Splash!* and the troll was never ever seen again. So me and the other two goats lived happily in the field. That is where I am now, retelling my exciting adventure to you.

Max Lever (9)
Glapton Primary & Nursery School, Nottingham

The Three Billy Goats Gruff

Dear Diary,

A couple of years ago me and my two brothers went over the bridge with a nasty old troll under it. This is what happened …

One sunny day my brothers and I had eaten all of the grass on the rocky side of the bridge, but we wanted more and wanted to go to the other side. So we decided and agreed my smaller brother should go first. He trotted across until he got to the middle, he stopped because the troll appeared. 'Who's that standing on my bridge?' the troll growled. The troll was going to eat him up, but he said he was too bony and the troll let him cross.

The same happened to my other brother, but when it was my turn I put my head down and ran and booted the troll into the air and he circled the sun and landed in the river and was never seen again.

As for me and my brothers we live on the other side of the field and cross the river whenever we want. See you.

Georgia Worrall (7)
Glapton Primary & Nursery School, Nottingham

Little Red Riding Hood Meets The Wolf

One summer's day my mum was making some cakes for my grandma. My grandma lived on the other side of the dark woods. In the woods there is a horrible and nasty wolf and whoever goes in doesn't always come back out.

When my mother gave me the basket of cakes it was time to go into the dark and gloomy woods. When I got to the start of the woods I knew I had to go in. When I took a step into the woods I heard footsteps racing through the woods. I was so scared so I just ran through. Then I knew my life was over because I saw the greedy wolf behind me, but all of a sudden my grandma came out of nowhere and shot the wolf with my grandad's shotgun. The bullet went straight through its heart. After my grandma had shot the wolf she shaved the wolf's coat and made a fur quilt cover for herself, and she sent the body to the poor.

Tyler Huthwaite (10)
Glapton Primary & Nursery School, Nottingham

The Three Little Pigs And The Big Bad Pig!

Once upon a time there were two ugly fat pigs called Perri and May who had a handsome brother Tom (who is me) and this is my story.

Two weeks ago an evil pig called Kelsy moved to the house next door and ate Perri and May, but I beat the snot out of Kelsy and he ran off and I never saw him again.

Thomas Knowles (11)
Glapton Primary & Nursery School, Nottingham

Dear Mr Wolf

Dear Mr Wolf,

We, the Forest Council, have heard that you have been terrorising the three pigs by demolishing their houses. If this happens again you will be fined with a £1,000,000 penalty. Only if it happens again, so be careful.

Dear Council,

Get your facts right! This never happened. What happened was I needed some sugar so I asked the pigs and then a high wind blew their house down.

Dear Mr Wolf,

We checked the forecast and it said it was going to be sunny all day so you will now lose £1,901,187 for lying, vandalism and destruction of other's property.

Scott Woolley (10)
Glapton Primary & Nursery School, Nottingham

Dear Sleeping Beauty

Dear Sleeping Beauty,

Your council tax has not been renewed yet and it has passed the deadline. If it isn't renewed quickly you will be fined £1,000. If that money doesn't come you will go to jail. There are different ways to pay the tax, one is to go to our website at www.payyourtax.com or phone us up on 0000 9852135 or finally come and pay at 69 Forest Lane NG15 9TB.

Yours sincerely
City Council.

Three weeks later.

Dear Sleeping Beauty,

So far we have not received your payment, so we are sending a removal team to take your furniture. If you don't let them in they will force entry.

Yours sincerely,
City Council.

James Brocklehurst (11)
Glapton Primary & Nursery School, Nottingham

The Three Little Pigs - Another Hungry Wolf!

Once upon a time there lived three little pigs. The three little pigs lived with their mother their whole lives. At one time, their mother turned round and said, 'You are getting too old to live with me now. Go off and find yourself a new house each.'

So the little pigs walked together down the road. All of a sudden the first little pig caught his eye on someone 'selling' boxes of chocolates for nothing. He thought, *hey, I can build my house out of chocolate.* So he got a couple of boxes and started to build. In a couple of minutes his house was done and dusted. He was so happy.

The second pig was jealous so he looked and found boxes of cornflakes. He got some boxes and started building his house. As quick as a racer, his house was up and done. He was pleased with his house.

The third pig was even more jealous so he looked around the village to see what he could find. He found different metals and started to build. As fast as lightning his house was done.

Out of the blue a wolf knocked on the chocolate coconut door and said, 'Little pig, little pig, please open the door.'

The pig replied, 'I don't think so! Do you think I am stupid?'

So the wolf melted the chocolate. The little pig ran to the second pig's house. The two little pigs shouted, 'Do not come near my house otherwise there will be trouble.'

The wolf started chomping on the cornflakes to get in. The two little pigs ran to the other house.

The three little pigs shouted, 'You won't be able to get in here.'

Did they get eaten or not?

Demi-Leigh Astill (10)
Glapton Primary & Nursery School, Nottingham

Eager To Eat

Dear Mr Wolf,

I am writing on behalf of myself that I understand that you have been harassing the nature including the three pigs. The three pigs will be grateful if you don't bother them anymore.

We have asked the three pigs whether you can make it up to them and they replied only if you promise not to be bad anymore and you can start off with remaking the houses that you have blown down and ruined.

After a while, there was no reply from the wolf. I decided to write to him and asked him whether he was ready to come round and rebuild the broken items, but there was no reply.

'Mr Wolf this can cause serious argumentative responses to our future but if you don't pay for the damage you will go to jail. The price is £1,000,000 if you don't pay you will be in serious trouble'.

Emma Savidge (11)
Glapton Primary & Nursery School, Nottingham

Witches' Spell Book

Fresh, slimy, grey snail's eyeballs.
Burning, scalding, steaming cat's tongue.
We won't see Sleeping Beauty she'll be locked beneath these
four walls.

Some mouldy maggots mixed with gruel.
Smelly sick mixed with rotten eggs.
It won't be Cinderella who will take over and rule.
Horrid, gross, unpleasant snot.
Revolting earwax smells like mouldy sewage.
I will kill Sleeping Beauty in my scalding-hot pot.

Louise Calvert (10)
Glapton Primary & Nursery School, Nottingham

Untitled

I was walking along the deep scary woods. I kept hearing the black evil wolf that's always tried to bite you and who'd creep up behind you.

I walked along and the wolf popped out right in front of me and I shot him right through the heart. I took the fur and made a coat.

Josh Kingsland (11)
Glapton Primary & Nursery School, Nottingham

Dear Mr Wolf

Fantasy Forest Council are writing to you on behalf of the Three Little Pigs as you've blown their house down. Unfortunately, they are scared, trembling, plus shaking like an earthquake. However, you will have to pay the price. Sadly, if an unpleasant person or something did it to you, you wouldn't like it. The prices for the houses are £1,000 for the house being built, £500 for each window (there are 4 windows), £40 for a door to be built and a handle, as well as £10,000 for all the rooms and £10,000 for all the furniture and other things.

Yours sincerely,
Fantasy Forest Council.

Dear Fantasy Forest Council

Why should I pay? I haven't done anything they dared me to, so they should move house or pay for it themselves. I'm sick of being accused of doing something I haven't done.

From,
Mr Wolf.

Sharna Francis (11)
Glapton Primary & Nursery School, Nottingham

Dear Little Red Riding Hood

Dear Little Red Riding Hood,

Are you aware that your attacker, the big bad wolf, has been fined and that all his victims are free and that he has been executed? So no worries now if you want help, don't hesitate to send us a letter. Furthermore, you will be compensated, your grandma has also been compensated. However, your grandma is suffering from shock, the minister for home defence has concluded that you can stay where you are or move in with your grandma. Whichever you decide is not our business. Moreover, it is our business to not interfere with relationships, we can put a full guard on your grandma's home if you grandma desires this then ask her to write a letter. Just before the wolf was executed we questioned him and he said Red Riding Hood was a nice girl even though we executed him. It was the electric chair we did it with.

From Josh Cook

Member of the Ministry for Home Defence.

Josh Cook (10)
Glapton Primary & Nursery School, Nottingham

Rhyme Of Red Riding Hood

One day in a house there was a little girl named Red Riding Hood. Her mum was not feeling well, she made her grandmother some apple pies. She said to Red Riding Hood, 'Take these pies to your gran's.'

So off she went into the wood. On her way she saw a wolf, the wolf said, 'I'll have her for my tea.'

So off he went to Gran's house and walked in, he put Gran in the smelly bin. Then the wolf went into the bed and Red Riding Hood came in the room, the wolf had a nasty grin on his face. She said, 'What furry hands you have.'

'Come closer to my bed dear.' He had a big smirk on his face.

'What big teeth you have.'

'I'll eat you for my tea.'

Bang!

The door came wide open, the smelly bin came in the room,I Gran's got the pie, *splat!* in the wolf's face. He went crying home to his mummy. The wolf was never to be seen again.

Amber Coles (8)
Glapton Primary & Nursery School, Nottingham

Dear Miss Red Riding Hood

Dear Miss Red Riding Hood,

I bet you've heard about the news in the newspaper. Thank you for being my pen pal. At least I have a friend to talk to. No one will listen or should I say believe my side of the story if I told you. I've got to go now, it is lunchtime, please send a letter back.

Love Mr Wolf.

Alison Brown (11)
Glapton Primary & Nursery School, Nottingham

Rhyme Of Red Riding Hood

One day in a little cottage there was a girl as good as gold and she was six years old. 'Red Riding Hood would you be a very good girl and take this crumble pie to your grandma's house because she's not well?'

Little Red put on her red hood and took a trip through the wood. When she passed by there was a wolf with a bad look in his eye. The wolf got to Grandma's house before Red Riding Hood and put Grandma in the bin. Red Riding Hood arrived. 'Come inside,' cried the wolf, so she opened the door very wide.

'What big teeth you have,' said Red Riding Hood. 'What big hands you have.'

'Come here so I can eat you.'

Just then Grandma chucked the crumble pie at the wolf and that was the last they saw of him.

Taylor Buck
Glapton Primary & Nursery School, Nottingham

Rhyme Of Red Riding Hood

One sunny morning there was a girl called Little Red Riding Hood. She was six years old and she was as good as gold.

'Go to your grandma's house because she is poorly and take this basket of food with you as well.'

So she got the basket and said goodbye. She went though the woods and there was a wolf. The wolf ran to Grandma's house, he put Grandma in the bin and closed the lid. He ran inside the house and got in bed. The door was wide open so she went inside and said, 'What big eyes you have.'

'Come a little closer.'

'What big teeth you have.'

He jumped out of bed and nearly grabbed her but Grandma whacked him and he ran away.

Jodi McQuade (9)
Glapton Primary & Nursery School, Nottingham

Reprincel

'What?' cried Princess Chloe.

'You will marry in three days, understand?'

'Yes Father,' she grumbled. Chloe had long black hair and was 21. That wasn't the only problem, she was cool, the princes weren't!

One day Chloe went riding on her horse. She came across a castle with a tall tower with one window at the top. She heard someone coming so she hid behind a huge bush. A witch appeared out of the forest and cried in a crackly voice, 'Reprincel, Reprincel, let down your hair!'

Strangely enough, the longest hair she'd ever seen (it was light brown) came tumbling down from the tower. A massive scaly dragon flew to the top of the tower, hovering by the window.

Meanwhile the witch climbed up the hair. When she got to the top, she went through the glassless window and out of sight. After about twenty minutes the witch came out, this time she went onto the dragon who had moved in front of the window.

When the witch had gone, Chloe came out of the rose bush, dismounted, then called up, 'Reprincel, Reprincel, let down your hair!'

Instantly the hair came down. She climbed up and went through the window. When she had a look at the tidy room she saw Reprincel and he said to her, 'What are you doing here?'

'Looking for you, now come on.'

When they escaped from the castle Chloe cut his hair and they were married.

Catriona Sutcliffe (8)
Gunthorpe CE Primary School, Nottingham

The Letter To Black & Decker

Dear Black & Decker,

I came in to your store last Wednesday, you know me, the woodcutter with the spiky hair.

Well, it started last Wednesday when I came in and bought a steel axe and it was not cheap! When I got home I put my tools in the van and the next day, when I got my axe out, I started to cut down the wood, so when I had cut it down I could sell it.

I kept on cutting wood. Well, I'm always cutting wood! But over the last few days I seemed to not notice that the blade has been going down when I've been cutting down the maple trees. So what are you going to do about it? A replacement would be good. It is not my fault that it's gone totally blunt!

When you get this letter call me on 107791 10341.

Yours sincerely

The Woodcutter.

Hugh Harland (9)
Gunthorpe CE Primary School, Nottingham

The Troll's Story Of The Billy Goats Gruff

One day, Toby the Troll was walking along the path. He went back home under the bridge. But when he got there, there was no black paint to paint the bridge.

The next day Mr Gruff was walking along the bridge. Toby jumped up but he scared Mr Gruff away and he thought that Toby was going to eat him. So he ran off. Toby said, 'Sorry, all I wanted to know is have you got any black paint?' But he didn't hear what he said.

Two hours later Mrs Gruff was trotting along to the butcher's across the bridge when the troll jumped up and said, 'Hello,' and then she ran away. Toby said, 'Wait, don't go away!'

At 6 o'clock in the evening Little Billy Goat Gruff was alone and then … Toby jumped up with a *bang!* Billy said, 'You don't scare me.'

'Don't I?' said Toby. 'Well I scared your mum and dad! Have you got any black paint?'

'Yes I have,' said Billy.

Mr and Mrs Gruff said, 'Leave him alone!'

'All I am asking him is if he's got any black paint!'

'Shut up!'

Then Mr Gruff came charging, then *bang!* His horns hit Toby on the bottom.

'All I was asking is if you've got any black paint!'

'Why didn't you say so?'

Then finally he got some and painted the bridge black. So that was the other side of the story.

Ryan Wetton-Byrne (9)
Gunthorpe CE Primary School, Nottingham

Bad Girl

News flash:

Bad girl, Goldilocks has broken into the three bears' house. We have the three bears live with us today. 'What do you think Mummy Bear?'

'I think it's awful she has come in and ruined my porridge, I took a long time to make that and we just went for a walk to let it cool down and she just had to come in and ate it all!'

'What a rude girl, but there is more. We have live with us Baby Bear.'

'Well, that little girl did not just eat our porridge, she came in the living room and sat on all the chairs! First she sat on Daddy's chair, I think she thought it was too hard because next she sat on Mummy's chair, but she thought that it was too soft, so she sat on my chair and guess what? That heavy little madam broke it! My lovely chair!'

'I am sorry Little Bear, about your chair. But we have one more person to speak to, that is Daddy Bear.'

'That little girl has come upstairs and slept in all of our beds. First mine and guess what? She had the cheek to say my bed was hard. *Hard? I'll give her hard!* That's why I chased her straight out of our house when we found her lying in Baby's bed. She's going to be made to pay for all the bills!'

'OK guys, thanks for coming. We will be back soon.'

Lydia Skerritt (9)
Gunthorpe CE Primary School, Nottingham

Billy Goats Gruff

Once upon a time there was a family of trolls, yes trolls, not goats, trolls! They wanted to get to the swamp over the hill, but there was one problem - the goat. He did not come out often, he would sit guarding the hill and make sure no one went over the hill, no one could beat him except The Super Gorilla of all time.

Sorry, sorry! Got a bit carried away. Anyway, boy did he give beef! When Gorilla went the goat came back. He wanted to get to the green fields, but the trolls wouldn't let him. So they made a deal and the trolls went to the swamp, the goat went to the green fields and The Super Gorilla lived on top of the hill. The goat had a family and they all lived happily ever after!

Joe Brownley (9)
Gunthorpe CE Primary School, Nottingham

Dear Barbra

Dear Barbra,

I have a slight problem … my tools have been ruined because I had to save a silly old granny out of wolf's tummy! I had to use my brand new golden axe and now I have a massive dent in it!

All my tools are destroyed by air-head princesses and pretty girls who pick flowers for their dear, sweet old grannies. I've had enough!

My sweet old granny got eaten by a big smelly bear named Big Bear, his identity card fell out of his pocket when he jumped out of the window trying to escape from me! My aunt is being surrounded by wolves and I need a new, sharp, golden saw!

Oh, and could you give me Red Riding Hood's phone number because I need a break! And I've heard she's pretty handy with an axe. I shall see you tomorrow or else! Sorry, I got carried away, I just love the action.

Well, um, could you ask Miss Riding Hood if she likes me because I've kind of got a crush on her! Forget that. Thanks mate

From

Kevin the Woodcutter.

Katy Southgate (9)
Gunthorpe CE Primary School, Nottingham

Dear Black & Decker

Dear Black & Decker,

I bought a saw from you last week and I used it once to cut open a wolf to get a granny out and now it's blunt! What can I do? I want my money back now!

I am going to tell all my friends not to come to you. The only time I am going to come to you now is to get the money back for the saw. You are rubbish! I will now only go to B&Q. I think I am going to ring the police. So you'd better be nice to me when I come!

Please call me when you get this letter on 10949 20748. Thank you.

The Woodcutter (from Little Red Riding Hood).

Jack Simms (9)
Gunthorpe CE Primary School, Nottingham

Mr And Mrs Bear

Dear Mr and Mrs Bear,

Your enemy Goldilocks has written a letter to us saying that Mrs Bear has cooked poisonous porridge and it has made her sick! She has also had to pay six hundred pounds just to have a plaster round her ankle, which she hurt when you chased her!

Mr Bear, she has complained because your bed made her have backache! And as for Baby Bear, she is complaining to the police because your chair broke and now Goldilocks has a sore bottom.

You are going to go to court on 19th June 2007 and it will start at 2pm. Just to let you know, Goldilocks will be there making a complaint. The judge will listen to both sides of the story, so don't shout at the judge because he will shout back at you and tell you to be silent. Goldilocks will go first to say what she has to say about what happened and then it will be your turn. I can't promise that you will get off lightly, you might have to go to prison!

Mr and Mrs Bear, I am sorry but you will only get off if Goldilocks doesn't press charges. But if she does, you will be sued!

See you on the 19th June 2007. Good luck, your solicitor will be there. It will be at Sun Hill.

Yours sincerely,
Goldilocks' Solicitor.

Charlotte Mayo (9)
Gunthorpe CE Primary School, Nottingham

The Real Story Of Goldilocks
And The Three Bears

Everyone thinks that they know the real story of Goldilocks and The Three Bears. Well, they think they do ... By the way their names are Ben, Beth and Bill. Bill is the baby, Beth is the mum and I am the dad, Ben. We are the bears and this is ...

The real story of Goldilocks and The Three Bears:

Mummy Bear was making porridge but it was so hot. So Mummy Bear and Daddy and Baby Bear all went for a walk. Then you know what happens after that! So we got our own back ...

All of us went to Goldilocks' house. Her mum had made some pizza, it was so hot! But Beth ate it all up. Then I went into the living room. There was an amazing chair there and on the label it said X2C. I did not know what it meant, but it was so big and red, so I sat on it. There were two more there.

Baby Bear was sick on all the beds So Goldilocks and her mum and dad could not sleep on them. Then we all heard the door open, so we all jumped out of the window and escaped!

Bethany Hampson-Smith (9)
Gunthorpe CE Primary School, Nottingham

Goldilocks And The Three Bears

Do you think that you know the story of Goldilocks and then think again? Why don't you take it from my point of view?

Well, Goldilocks was in the wood, she was picking flowers for almost an hour, she looked up and sniffed the air but really she did not care. By and by in the woods she came across Miss Red Riding Hood, they seemed to fit, she went to a house and had some cereal, one hot, one cold.

She sat down on one armchair, it was too big, one too soft and one too small, so she broke it, I think. She went upstairs to try to think, she flopped onto a filthy bed. She was drowsy and she didn't care about the bears. One little one, one middle-sized, one big. Little Bear said, 'Come on, let's go home.'

'No, we've only just got here,' said Mummy Bear with glaring eyes. He ran off through the wood and Mummy Bear went after him. 'Come back!' she said and dashed away.

Goldilocks was very quiet and when Baby Bear was looking over her she opened her eyes and said, 'Argh,' and screamed out loud, with a pistol she aimed at all three! *Bang! Bang! Bang!* She shot them dead.

On the news I heard them say, today the bears didn't have their prey!

Amy Keane (8)
Gunthorpe CE Primary School, Nottingham

The True Story Of Little Red Riding Hood

Everyone knows the story of Little Red or they think they do! *That's not the real story!* The reporters wanted to jazz it up, adding a bit more gore! How disgusting saying the woodcutter chopped me in half to get Granny out!

I am Mr John Dickson George Wire - you can call me John. The real story is about a bad shock and a frightened Granny …

The true story!

I was snoozing behind a tree when an ignorant little miss sneaked up and went, *'Boo!'* I didn't realise at first, she had a basket of daffodils. I wouldn't have shown my teeth if I'd known! It was too late! She ran screaming to her granny's house. Granny happens to be my friend.

Granny had her own problems, she'd eaten a crumb of the woodcutter's cake and he'd gone bonkers, chasing her with his shiny golden axe. As you can imagine Granny put on her running shoes and legged it all the way home. When Granny got home I was there (she'd given me a spare key!) 'Wolfie, help? Because I've stolen a bit of cake, the woodcutter's going to chop me in half! I need to hide!'

Now I'm easily shocked and of course my mouth shot open!

'Good idea Wolfie, you're a genius! I'll hide in your mouth.'

I was shouting stop, but it was too late! Little Red arrived screaming, as Granny hopped in. That attracted the woodcutter and I went to jail.

That's the true story!

Georgia Simpson (8)
Gunthorpe CE Primary School, Nottingham

The True Story Of The Three Little Pigs, The Wolf's Side Of The Story!

I bet you think that you know the true story of The Three Little Pigs? But you don't. So if you have a copy of it just say goodbye and then put it in the bin, put a lid on the bin and lock it!

Have I introduced myself? Well, if I didn't my name is Mr A Idiot. But I would rather be called Angus. I am here to tell you the *true story of The Three Little Pigs.* Trust me, they really were pigs! Welcome to my side of the story.

I was just making some pancakes because it was Shrove Tuesday, when I realised that I had no flour. So I went to my next-door neighbour (who was the First Little Pig) and said, 'Little Pig number one, do you wish to kindly donate some flour to me?'

'No Mr Angus Idiot,' the pig replied. All of a sudden I felt my bum wriggling until I did an enormous trump! When all the green smoke had disappeared, I saw the pig right in the middle of what was, but isn't anymore, a house! Dead as a post he was! So I thought he wouldn't mind me looking through the ruins of his house for some flour! But the silly pig didn't have any …

Jemma Mills (9)
Gunthorpe CE Primary School, Nottingham

The Real Story Of Little Red Riding Hood

Once upon a time, me, the wolf that is, well I was having a little snooze like I always do on a Saturday morning. The birds were tweeting up in the trees, a gentle fresh breeze blowing through my fur, no disturbances. I woke up then stretched and yawned and yawned and stretched a little more. I stood up and wiped the sleep from my eyes, then shook the sleepiness right out of me. I was just about to go back to picking flowers for my granny when I saw there was a human. You know, a daughter of Eve. I wandered over to ask her what her name was when she quite rudely said, 'Go away and leave me alone, I am not allowed to talk to strangers!'

What rudeness, then she told me that she was picking flowers for her granny too. So I tell you what I did. All I did was ask her what her name was and where her granny lived and what did she say? Absolutely zilch!

So I followed her. Along the curvy cobbled lane, up a steep grassy hill, then she knocked on the door. I hid behind the tree on the left of the house. Before she got in I snuck round the back and Granny was so scared she ran away …

Amy Frogson (9)
Gunthorpe CE Primary School, Nottingham

Jessica And Rapunzel

One dark winter's night a man named Charlie went into a witch's garden to get some vegetables for himself and his wife. As Charlie was picking some carrots, he got scared because a crunchy noise got louder and louder behind him. Suddenly something touched his shoulder. 'You thief,' whispered a voice.

There was an awful smell in the garden. Charlie turned round, surprised by the witch. Charlie tried not to scream but made a little squeak. Charlie stood silently looking at the witch. The silence was broken by the sound of the witch's dreadful squeaky voice. 'What are you doing?' she screamed at Charlie.

'Err … well … nothing,' said Charlie.

'Hmm,' said the witch, 'well why have you got my vegetables then?' she said calmly.

'My wife is having twins and she needs something to eat,' said Charlie.

'You may have the vegetables, but when the twins are born they will belong to me!' cackled the witch.

Two weeks later the twins were born. Charlie and his wife Clair were scared of the witch. They thought the witch had forgotten about them. Later the witch turned up. 'Where are the twins?' said the witch. She snatched the twins off Clair and ran away. Sixteen years later, the witch built a tower to lock the twins in. Their names were Jessica and Rapunzel.

The witch never let Rapunzel and Jessica cut their hair because she put chains on the door of the tower so nobody could take them and so they could not get away. Each day the witch would shout, 'Rapunzel, Jessica, let down your hair.' So they'd let down their hair. They let down their hair so the witch could climb up. She would give them their food then go back to her house and hide. In the tower the girls sang lovely sad songs …

Kelsi Lucas (8)
Gunthorpe CE Primary School, Nottingham

Little Red Riding Wolf

Once upon a time there was a wolf called Little Red Riding Wolf and a girl called Little Red Riding Hood, a Granny called Anne and a woodcutter called Bill Bob.

Once upon a time I was a wolf called Wolf Riding Hood but you can call me Wolfie. Now do you know the story of Little Red Riding Hood and the big bad wolf? The true story? Only I know it! I was not a big bad wolf, I was actually a good wolf. Red Riding Hood was bad, I tell you! I do not know how to explain this big bad thing, but I am going to tell you the real story. The story of Little Red Riding Wolf.

One day I was picking flowers for my granny, when I don't know how to explain it, a girl wrecked my flowers. I was going to get her back! But how? I asked her where she was going. She said, 'My grandma's'.

I asked, 'Where does your gran live?'

'Six Acre Close.'

I went to her gran's house and ate her gran up and gobbled her up. I was chopped in half and that was the end of me!

Courtney Abell (8)
Gunthorpe CE Primary School, Nottingham

Little Red Riding Hood

Once upon a time there was a girl called Red Riding Hood and she was going to visit her sweet old granny. Little Red Riding Hood's mum said to her, 'Can you take these beautiful flowers from the forest?'

So Little Red Riding Hood went into the forest and picked some flowers, she had some currant buns with her. 'Hello Red Riding Hood, where are you going today?' said the wolf.

'I am going to visit my sweet old granny and I have got her some sweet flowers and currant buns to eat. Granny are you in?' said Little Red Riding Hood. No answer. So Little Red Riding Hood went in. 'Where are you Granny, because I have brought you some flowers and some currant buns.'

Little Red Riding Hood went into her granny's bedroom. Granny was in bed but it wasn't Granny, it was the wolf. 'Where's my granny?'

'Sorry, I have eaten her.'

Red Riding Hood phoned the woodcutter and he came to chop the wolf up and he got Red Riding Hood's granny out.

Lewis Mayo (8)
Gunthorpe CE Primary School, Nottingham

Dear Mr Wolf

Dear Mr Wolf,

Why did you eat my grandma? What point was there of breaking into her house? And oh yeah, Black & Decker are angry they've wasted their tools on you. They have to pay £20 to the woodcutter. You've been fined £1,000. You have to pay by the end of the week.

My grandma told me that she was very scared. She wishes you don't return. You will be in jail for two years and I'm very happy that you're going to jail.

Yours truly

Little Red Riding Hood.

Adam Deverill (9)
Gunthorpe CE Primary School, Nottingham

Goldilocks And The Three Bears

Once upon a time there lived three sneaky bears and a girl called Goldilocks. One day the three bears went to Goldilocks' house, luckily she was on her morning walk so the bears went in and had a look.

The three bears saw some porridge and ate it. When they had finished they went for a walk in the park. Soon after they'd had a walk in the park then they went back to Goldilocks' house.

When they got back they felt a little tired so they went upstairs. As soon as they got upstairs they saw three beds, so Daddy Bear went in the big bed, Mummy Bear went in the medium-sized bed and Little Bear went in the small bed. Suddenly the door opened and in a rush they jumped out of the window and were never seen again.

Callum Slack (8)
Gunthorpe CE Primary School, Nottingham

Little Red Riding Hood's Grandma

Dear Fairy Godmother,

Please help me I am stuck in a bad wolf's tummy. Because he just decided to gobble me up! I asked him not to, but he just ignored me and unfortunately ate me.

Please mix a potion to get me out please! I did not do anything to him. All I was doing at the time was lying in bed. It just barged in and gobbled me up.

Please help!

From Red Riding Hood's Grandma.

Catherine Angus (8)
Gunthorpe CE Primary School, Nottingham

Dear Mr Wolf

Dear Mr Wolf,

I bet you weigh a ton from eating those poor two little pigs. I don't know where you put the other one, but I want him back. *Please* come to the Nottingham court at 10am tomorrow

Yours sincerely,

PC Stevens

PS If I catch you eating any more pigs you're in big trouble.

Dear PC Stevens,

I am not coming to Nottingham court and I don't weigh a ton thank you very much! Sorry about the trouble.

From Mr Wolf.

Ava Stevens (7)
Gunthorpe CE Primary School, Nottingham

Little Red Riding Hood

One day a wolf named Little Red Riding Wolf woke up and the wolf had just had a dream about a human granny …

Well, you see it started like this … he woke up in a human house being adored by a human. Got out of bed, went through an open window then an old granny gave him a kiss. Not just any old kiss. It was a big slippery kiss! So the wolf ended up with a massive patch of lipstick on his fur!

Suddenly he woke up in the house and ran out of the front door and straight into a metal trap that shut like a sharp pair of jaws. He did what wolves do! *Awwooooooo!*

The family heard him. They suddenly rushed out and brought him to the vet. He had to be put into a cage because he had a broken leg. The wolf could not walk for a long time on his leg and it got infected.

When his leg had healed he was let out into the wild. He found the rest of his family in a forest, feasting on a family of rabbits. By the time they had finished their rabbit dinner they had to go into their den to go to sleep.

Jordan Slack (8)
Gunthorpe CE Primary School, Nottingham

Little Red Riding Wolf

You may recall the story of Little Red Riding Hood, but this is the real version.

In once upon a time land, there was a wolf. That wolf lived on his own. His only living relative was his punk rocker grandma, Florence. She gave Little Red Riding Wolf chocolate every day. So as you can imagine Little Red Riding Wolf was fat … wrong! He was as skinny as can be. You could see his bones and hear his groans and … oh let's get on with the story.

That day, Little Red Riding Wolf made a cake to take to his punk rocker grandma. As he approached his grandma's door he heard a noise. *What could it be?* he wondered. *What could it be?* He entered …

He could not speak as the cake fell to the ground. His grandma's house was shaking. She was playing her guitar. Little Red Riding Wolf joined in. Just at that moment he noticed the drummer, it was the Big Bad … Squirrel?

Tyler Guy (10)
Heathfield Primary School, Nottingham

The True Story Of Humpty Dumpty

Humpty Dumpty sat on a wall. A really, really high wall. When a storm brewed he got hit by lightning and he fell and fell and fell and fell and fell and fell until … *crack!* All the king's horses and all the king's men had eggs for breakfast, lunch and dinner again and again and again. The sad but true end.

Antonio Palinczuk (10)
Heathfield Primary School, Nottingham

Three Little Pigs

Dear Three Little Pigs,

I am so sorry for the disruption that I have caused to your houses by blowing them down. My actions were unacceptable, I don't know what came over me and I truly hope that you will forgive me and accept my apologies (but I don't know why you had to call the police).

You and your brothers really hurt me by pushing me into that cooking pot. It still hasn't stopped hurting my tail even though 55 years have gone by.

I would ask of you that you pay the fine to release me from prison.

Signed

Mr Wolf.

PS I wouldn't be surprised if you were to turn down my apology.

Hannah Musovic (10)
Heathfield Primary School, Nottingham

The Three Little Pigs

So there I was minding my own business when suddenly a big bad wolf bursts in on me. My poor little house was a pile of straw. I could not bear it anymore, I fainted and I fell to the floor. When he was about to eat me I woke up. I smacked him one and ran next door.

I sat down, had a cup of tea and we met again. He burst through the kitchen door and when he found me there was more trouble. My brother and I, we shivered and quivered as he blew our house down and I mean *right down!* Nothing left but a pile of sticks. So we ran to the house of bricks.

I was laying down now, tired as ever, when once again he came round in the pouring rain. Drenched as he was, but still tough though still not strong enough. I'd built up courage and walked up with a slap and a punch. I beat him up and that was the end of the big bad wolf.

Rowan Sipson (10)
Heathfield Primary School, Nottingham

The Death Of Flumpety

It was stuck! He grabbed at it. The scarf stuck round the nail. He toppled off the wall. Was he dead?

There was a lot of confusion in Clumpety town. Was this harmless egg pushed? Flumpety was definitely brain dead. The little egg lay there surrounded by puddles of egg yolk and white. Flumpety's scarf was frayed, tattered and torn. Its all-over pattern was a bundle of shreds. It was taken for forensic science investigation in the leggboratory.

Three days later the shock was down but the town was still quiet. The family of Flumpety couldn't eat, sleep or even bear to wash.

The funeral was flowery with eggs. Eggs were placed in his eggshell grave.

Many years passed and Flumpety's family still grieve but they're over the worst, now they're with him, dead.

It was an accident, hopefully.

Katie Ridley (10)
Heathfield Primary School, Nottingham

Rapunzel

My wife and I lived in a nice house in a nice area, although the only problem was the next-door neighbour, believe it or not. She was really (an old hag), she wasn't exactly a friend to us. She had no husband and no children and no friends. Anyway, back to the basics.

When my wife was pregnant and about to give birth then the old hag came round and said, 'When your wife has that baby then give the baby to me or your wife will never see the living daylights ever,' she cackled.

So when my wife had given birth we had to give her away. Every night when I go in the forest I see her peering out of the window and I hear the old hag say, 'Rapunzel, Rapunzel, let down your hair so I can climb without a stair'.

One night I saw a white horse and a man jump off it. He walked to the window and shouted, 'Rapunzel, Rapunzel, let down your hair.' She let him climb up and the one thing I didn't know was that she was getting married the following day.

Jade Unwin (11)
Heathfield Primary School, Nottingham

Marshmallow Nightmare

Once upon a time I was in Heaven. I was lying down on the white soft cloud. Suddenly a huge marshmallow came flying down from skies above. I started chomping it. Mmm … chicken.

I woke up and half of the pillow was gone. Pillow fluff was all over my face!

Aimen Arshad (11)
Henry Whipple Junior School, Nottingham

Untitled

I turned and ran with the ball. I ran down the right side. I crossed the ball into Davis. Goaalllll!

The keeper dived the wrong way. He had no chance of saving it. England 1 Ecuador 0. Camera flashes, St George's flags all around. The crowd were singing as one voice.

Jak Hamilton (10)
Henry Whipple Junior School, Nottingham

Small Task

We were at a dance competition and me and my partner were up next. As we got onto the dance floor the music started … My partner spun me around like a doughnut. Then he lifted me like an angel. I could feel the tension lift, and we won the competition.

Shelby Kerry (11)
Henry Whipple Junior School, Nottingham

The Bloodthirsty Dragon

One night in a dark swamp there was a bloodthirsty dragon. He had massive claws. His eyes were luminous yellow. His breath smelt like rotten flesh. He was lurking in the swamp. He saw flashing lights. He wanted to find out what it was so he went thumping down the dark street.

Unfortunately everybody was asleep except one boy. The boy couldn't sleep. He heard thumping down the street. He got out of his bed and peeked out of the window. Suddenly he saw the ugly fierce dragon. The boy was petrified.

Suddenly the dragon put his gigantic head through the window. The gobsmacked boy ran to the door. It was locked. The dragon sank his jaws into his legs and swallowed him whole.

Kerry Bonser (11)
Henry Whipple Junior School, Nottingham

The World Cup

I am very scared. I am shaking. My heart is beating fast. I hear the other team laughing evilly. I can hear the England crowd, 'Come on, England!'

We are going to win. Whistle goes. I walk out on the pitch …

Rebekha Bedding (11)
Henry Whipple Junior School, Nottingham

The Spectacular Goal

There I was with the ball under my feet. There was nothing I could do but shoot.

Suddenly a player came, I chipped it over him and minutes left. I had a shot and scored, everyone was overjoyed. We won the tournament. It was a spectacular trophy.

George Tomlinson (11)
Henry Whipple Junior School, Nottingham

The Best World Cup Ever

The manager told us to get out there and win the World Cup for all the fans and football lovers.

I went to take a penalty. I could hear my heart hitting my ribs. Goaaalll!

I ran across the pitch amazed.

Adam Bellamy (11)
Henry Whipple Junior School, Nottingham

Small Talk

I was there the last minute of the game. Still 0-0, I had the ball, suddenly my stomach churned so I ran and ran. I was ready. 10 seconds left I was sweating. I put all my power in to it. I scored. *Goalll*! We won the World Cup! *Yesss!*

Mathew Whittaker (11)
Henry Whipple Junior School, Nottingham

The Shadow

The boy is silently asleep in his bed when suddenly a shadow appears at the door. The boy wakes up and sees the shadow at the door. It moves closer to him. The boy hides under his sporty quilt. *Crack, creak* as the shadow walks.

He realises it's his dad!

Adam Lockwood (10)
Milbrook Primary School, Grove

The Ticking In The Night

I was in bed at the time. I heard a tick-tock. The door creaked open. I would've run. But I was frozen. The lights flickered twice and turned on. I saw an ugly face approaching me. The face of my brother. 'What's the time?' he asked. I said nothing.

Dominic Thackray (10)
Milbrook Primary School, Grove

The Story

My hands trembled. I glanced at the clock. 20 minutes. I started to write. Time ticked by. I sighed, flopping back on my chair, and crossed out the first few words. 15 minutes. I knew I was never going to do it. I would never win the competition.

Gaby Beckley (9)
Milbrook Primary School, Grove

Illusion

One night a boy was lying in the dark in his bedroom. He heard a noise and woke up. 'What was that?' he said.

Creak, creak.

There was another noise. He heard a clatter. He saw a shadow. He was really scared.

'Phew,' it was just an illusion.

Shane Harris (10)
Milbrook Primary School, Grove

The Battle Of Hastings

There we were, both tribes getting ready to fight. The first soldier stepped forward. 'Charge!'

There were dying cries coming from every angle, then I saw three soldiers. All three spears were pointing at me, they charged at me, full speed.

I woke with sweat dripping down my face.

Thomas Fell (10)
Milbrook Primary School, Grove

Surprise

I was in the car and Mum and Dad were not talking to me, and not telling me where we were going. My parents were being really mean, they must be going shopping, that's really boring.

Suddenly we stopped, we were at the seaside, my favourite place. The wonderful seaside.

Maxwell Williams (10)
Milbrook Primary School, Grove

Spooks Will

There were two girls having sleepovers. They heard a knock at the window, they hid under the covers. Then when they thought it was safe they came up to the surface. Then they saw a shadow run past the door.

They ran upstairs.

Mum said it was the cat.

Abbie Ellis (10)
Milbrook Primary School, Grove

The Black Stranger

Suddenly the door swung open, there stood a man. From head to foot, he was dressed in black. He stared, stared, at the child, at the mother, at the room.

Slowly he moved his gaze from the room and said, 'Sorry, wrong house.' His voice was shrill as he left.

Deborah Martin (10)
Milbrook Primary School, Grove

The White Light

Once there was a young man who'd just moved house. He wanted to see his old house one last time. He opened the door and saw an extremely bright light, saying, 'It's two in the morning.'

It was a grumpy horrible old lady in a very bright white dressing gown.

George Audas (9)
Milbrook Primary School, Grove

Scream!

Becci was in bed when she heard a smash. Then she heard a scream, so she shouted for her mum. Her mum came, Becci told her mum what had happened. Her mum said that it was teenagers in the street being stupid. The scream was a baby crying.

Paige Watts (10)
Milbrook Primary School, Grove

Television Out

There was a dreadful thunderstorm. There was a scary movie on the TV. There were people in a temple.

Mum went to get some popcorn. She left the remote under a cushion. When Mum came back the TV flickered and suddenly went out.

Mum had sat on the remote!

Luke Kirkland (9)
Milbrook Primary School, Grove

Panic

The plane was gaining altitude. The skydiver jumped out. His parachute bag fell off. He was falling rapidly to the ground.

Suddenly, the unthinkable happened.

He hit the ground. The most experienced skydiver woke up and realised he had fallen off his bed!

Timothy Cloete (10)
Milbrook Primary School, Grove

I Heard A Noise

Once I was walking in the night, when I heard a noise. I panicked. Then I saw this beautiful bird. It was an owl. The owl flew out of the tree as happy as can be. Why was I scared after all? Then I had a peaceful walk.

Ian Cotton (10)
Milbrook Primary School, Grove

The Worry

I was smashing through the trees, with sweat running down my back, my eyes were not moving. Then I came to a tiger, just standing there. When I touched it, it roared at me. I turned the corner and lurking there was a boy. How exciting was that play area!

Luke Parsons (10)
Milbrook Primary School, Grove

Oh No!

My heart thudded, sweat dripped off my fingertips. My stomach had butterflies and my spine was tingling. Going round gave me a headache, a killing headache. My eyes were going blurry seeing the same view all the time.

I can't believe I'm scared of merry-go-rounds. Oh no!

Robyn Grundy (10)
Milbrook Primary School, Grove

The Mystery

A cold shiver went down their spine, his legs turned to stone. He thought they would be eaten by a bear. They got in the car. 'No! We're out of petrol.' The dad went to find some. When he got back his son and wife had gone …

Alex Frost (10)
Milbrook Primary School, Grove

Intruder

I was getting undressed ready for bed, when my light started flickering. I was terrified. I hid. It must have been an intruder. Listening. I got out of bed very cautiously. I tiptoed to my light. I realised my light bulb had blown. There was no intruder.

Paige Aitken (10)
Milbrook Primary School, Grove

The Greyhound House Ghost

One night at Greyhound Hotel, when everybody was asleep, all of a sudden … 'Argh!' Everyone awoke. There were screams, flickering lights, it went on for hours. Everyone's shaking until it stopped. They looked and all of a sudden, 'Rrrrggggh!'

A little boy had a sheet over him!

Gemma Tuckey (10)
Milbrook Primary School, Grove

Late At Night

One night a girl woke up because she heard a ticking, she was really scared because there was no clock in her room. She tiptoed across the landing but there was no clock. She crept downstairs and peered round the curtain, to find a newly born bird waiting for its feed.

Abbie Norton (10)
Milbrook Primary School, Grove

Late In The Night

One night a girl was in bed and she heard someone downstairs. It wasn't her parents they'd gone out to dinner, it wasn't the babysitter - she had already gone home. She heard a man's voice.

'It must be a burglar!'

She tiptoed downstairs and found the telly had been left on.

Amy Brazier (10)
Milbrook Primary School, Grove

The Demon Cat!

One night a boy called Okhan awoke from a deep slumber. He saw something moving in the shadows, he decided to investigate, armed with a plastic sword. He turned around and came face to face with a demon cat! The black demon pounced, it was his cat Tiddles.

Jake Griffin (10)
Milbrook Primary School, Grove

The Nightmare Dream

'Help me, help me, I'm falling.'

I was getting closer and closer to the ground, by now all I could see was a dark, black floor with puddles of blood shining over it. It was getting darker and colder, then I heard my mum, and realised it was a dream.

Pippa Peart (10)
Milbrook Primary School, Grove

The Howling Noise

It was a cold, blustery Hallowe'en, there was a full, glowing moon and the werewolves were out! I was in a deep sleep. Suddenly I was awoken by … a werewolf, in my house! I crept downstairs and I was attacked by my puppy licking me!

Emily Smith (10)
Milbrook Primary School, Grove

Monster

'Aaarggghh!' I screamed as I ran upstairs. 'Gotta hide, gotta hide!'
    'I'm coming,' bellowed the monster.
    'Aaargggghhh!' I couldn't keep my mouth shut.
    'Here you are!' screeched the monster. 'I've found you!'
    'Aaargggghhh!' again I screamed. 'Not a bath!'

Joshua Woodbridge (10)
Milbrook Primary School, Grove

Spooked Out

Squeak!

What was that! I trembled. I looked around. Then I saw something terrifying! I saw something with a cane-like tail and egg-shaped head, and micro dishes for ears! I fainted.

At last I woke up. I saw it again. 'Aarrgghhh!'

I looked closer. It was a mouse.

Kieran Pope (10)
Milbrook Primary School, Grove

The Dragon

Whoosh!

I manoeuvred my broomstick away from the dragon. Its enormous wings crashed behind me. I turned to look how close it was and crashed. I fell and hit the floor. I started to run and tripped. I saw the dragon looming behind.

'Wow! I like this book!'

Jack Wellstood (10)
Milbrook Primary School, Grove

Hide-And-Seek

'Help, aaargghh! Where shall I hide?'
   'Jimmy, where are you?'
   'Oh no! I know, under my bed.'
   'Ready or not, Jimmy!'
   'Oh no, he's in the room.'
   'Jimmy, I see you.'
   'Nnnnooooo!'
   'Yes it's me! It's your turn to count! Finally!'

Jay Thomas (10)
Milbrook Primary School, Grove

The Zebra And The Lion

One day there was a lion going to pounce on a zebra. *Snap!* The lion stepped on a twig, the zebra ran for its life. Then the zebra fell over, the lion took its chance and pounced on it.

'I love this game!' said the little girl to her brother.

Rebecca Warboys (9)
Milbrook Primary School, Grove

The Burglar

At midnight I looked across the room. I saw a strange head and stripy clothes, at first it looked like a strange man. I walked towards him, he swung his arm at me fiercely, and then I realised it was my pyjamas blowing from side to side.

Joshua Patrick (10)
Milbrook Primary School, Grove

The Noise From Downstairs

One night a girl called Lucy went to bed. Suddenly she heard a noise from downstairs. She tiptoed down and her heart was beating faster than a drum. She opened the kitchen door and came face to face with a monster …

It was the fridge!

Rhiannon Hurst (10)
Milbrook Primary School, Grove

Money Mayhem

'Hand over the money!' whispers Skillz.

'I told you I don't have it,' says Jazz.

'What's in the briefcase? It's the money! Do you know what I'm going to do to you, I'm ...'

'Boys, time for tea!'

'Let's finish the game later,' said Charlie.

Alice Cox (9)
Milbrook Primary School, Grove

The Scare!

I was trekking through the jungle, I was being followed. Suddenly - *whoosh!* I felt an arrow shoot past my ear. I was acting like a ninja. I was a ninja! More arrows were shot at me, I awoke with a start. I won't fall asleep in front of the television.

Maia Sprules (10)
Milbrook Primary School, Grove

Noises In The Night

I was peacefully lying in my bed when suddenly I heard a growl, then a rustle of footsteps. I froze. I struggled down in my covers, 'Who's there?' Sweat trickled down my cheek, my heart was thudding madly. The door creaked open. Help!

Silly me, it was only my dog.

Yasmin Bahar (10)
Milbrook Primary School, Grove

The Sound

I was in my room then I heard this sound. So I walked downstairs. I started walking to the door then I heard this tremendous shout. So I ran in and it was just my dad watching football. I went back upstairs and I went to sleep.

Tyler Curtis (9)
Milbrook Primary School, Grove

Barking Mad

I was surrounded by thousands of them, yapping, trying to get in my pockets. I tried to get away but more of them came. Then suddenly, *bang!* I found myself in my bedroom, and I heard little noises. I looked down at the floor, and there were my small puppies.

Sara Coakley (9)
Milbrook Primary School, Grove

The Royal Button

A state of emergency has been declared as the Queen has lost her royal button. There is a £50,000 reward at stake for the first person to return the button. For many months now we have been a very sad kingdom, the crops have failed and the Queen is very, very upset and angry. So she raised the taxes. *Now my best friend is a lonely shoemaker and has not very much money, only enough to pay his taxes and none for food!*

One dull Tuesday afternoon I saw something shining in the corner of my eye. What was it I wondered?

It was the Royal Button!

So I rushed right over to it. So as soon as I personally gave the Queen her Royal Button and got the reward, I gave my poor friend the reward!

Josh Gillott (10)
Rampton Primary School, Retford

The Wise Old Tree

In my garden sits a wise old tree, towering over my house. I climb the tree every day.

But one day, the wind blew, and my tree stumbled down.

What was I to do?

Sarah Hinds (9)
Rampton Primary School, Retford

The Robbery

George crept through the guarded hotel searching for the golden safe. Approaching the room he spotted the safe placed on the dressing table. One, four, six, his secret password revealed the medallion. He found the door, he was prepared, it slowly opened.

There were flashing lights. Police. He was arrested.

George Frank (10)
Sonning Common Primary School, Reading

Payback

Fifty squawking crows flew over head. Suddenly *bang!* One bird plunged to the ground. Again, *bang!* Two birds lay dead on the moors.

The man holding his smoking shotgun gathered them up and settled down to eat his lunch. He squinted skywards. *Splat!* Something white landed in his sandwich. Payback!

Matthew Outram (10)
Sonning Common Primary School, Reading

My Underground Adventure

One glorious summer day I was walking along a shaded path, when I stumbled into a deep hole. But when I got up and dusted myself off I found that I was in another layer. All around me were cauldrons and potion bullets, weird substances and lots of books. On a table in the far corner of the room was a spell, written in fancy writing. I read it silently in my head. This is what it said: *'How to get out of difficult spaces. Ingredients: 56 rat tails, 77 spiders legs and 100 cats hairs'*.

'I know, I'll use the spell,' I said to myself. So I looked around the room for the ingredients. When I eventually found them, I tipped them into an empty cauldron and stirred them together. Then I found an old drinking goblet and poured the mixture inside. 'Here goes nothing,' I said as I drank the murky-coloured substance.

I felt as if I were moving, but I could not open my eyes. It was like someone had glued them together. Suddenly I felt a bump and I could open my eyes again. I was back on the pathway.

'It's good to be back,' I said to myself as I started to walk away.

Sophie Lewis (10)
Sonning Common Primary School, Reading

The Romantic Spider!

A spider was in a pathway in the middle of nowhere. There was a young lad on the path. The spider looked ferocious as though she was oozing with evil. He was a sensation. She was mesmerised and transfixed. The young lad swaggered towards her, slipping her a delicious fly!

Jacob Lee (11)
Sonning Common Primary School, Reading

Love On The Bus

There was a chap, he was travelling on a bus. There was a lass,, travelling on the same bus. She was beautiful.

He was writing frantically. She seemed dazzled by his charms. He seemed not to have noticed. As she got off, he slipped a love poem into her coat.

Robert Kenrick (11)
Sonning Common Primary School, Reading

Teacher Of Horror

Sophie was excited as she was starting a new year, with a new class and a new teacher. Sophie had been told her new teacher was very kind. Still thinking about her new teacher, Sophie reached her school. She sat next to her best friend Milly. At that moment Sophie's teacher walked in and wrote her name on the board. It read 'Miss Muffin'. 'Where's your reading books?' she shouted fiercely.

Immediately everyone got their reading books out and kept their heads down. Anyone who didn't get their reading books out was sent to the headmaster. Every lesson Miss Muffin taught she sent someone to the headmaster or shouted at the class.

For lunch Miss Muffin made worm sandwiches and made the children eat them. Sophie's best friend was sick so Miss Muffin smacked her with a ruler and she started to cry. When the clock ticked home time, everyone in Miss Muffin's class ran as fast as they could, out of the door, across the playground and home.

The next day Sophie was thinking of a plan to get rid of Miss Muffin. When Miss Muffin came in Sophie and the class tied her to a chair. They smacked her with a ruler, made her eat worm sandwiches and told the headmaster what she had been doing. When the children went back to class, the window was open and the ropes were untied …

Amy Chadwick (10)
Sonning Common Primary School, Reading

The Final Fall

Dear Diary,

I am revealing my secret to you of how I died. It was a lovely hot day so I decided to go for a picnic. I got all my bags ready and set off. After a while I found a good solid red brick wall to sit on. So I climbed on to it and started to unpack. You would never have thought that Miss Muffet would rudely knock me off while she was running away from the hairy spider. I smashed into a billion pieces. Luckily Miss Red Riding Hood was there to run to a phone box to tell the king to send his men on horses, to put me back together again. I will never forget her kindness. But they couldn't fix me, so I am still here, dying slowly. I am ... afraid ... this ... is ... the ... last ... time ... I ... will ... write ... my ... d ... i ... a ... r ...y.

George Maxted (10)
Sonning Common Primary School, Reading

Dear Sir/ Madam

Dear Sir/ Madam,

I am writing to you to complain about the issues that have been happening to me. I am fed up and tired of that kid Jack and the giant who are climbing up me. If this keeps happening to me I will fall down.

It will take 6 months for me to grow as tall as I am now. I am so old and my leaves are very delicate. For three days running he has been climbing up me, but I don't know why. I mean what is he going to find up there? 2 days ago he climbed down with a pot of glittering gold coins. The sack swayed from side to side and knocked some of my leaves off.

Yesterday he came down with a horrible harp. The strings caught in my leaves. And today he brought a furious hen down. Every time it laid an egg it landed on my roots and turned into golden goo.

Suddenly a large giant came out of nowhere and with it half a dozen of my leaves. The pain was unbearable, could you put a preservation order on me so in the meantime I am protected?

Yours faithfully,
The Beanstalk.

Ben Sharpe (10)
Sonning Common Primary School, Reading

Dear Diary

Dear Diary,

That woman is pure evil. She has something against me but I don't know what. OK she's my stepmum but this isn't a fairy tale!

First she goes and gets a woodcutter to kill me. Unfortunately for him I'm a black belt at Judo. When I found a house to live in with all these small men she managed to find me, the old cow, and then she nearly killed me with a poisoned apple. Those little men didn't help either. They assumed I was dead so dug a hole and put me in it. Fortunately after I coughed out the apple in my sleep I put my rock climbing skills to use. My arms may be skinny but boy are they useful.

Soon after I climbed out the hole a prince came riding by. Wasn't a very handsome guy but still he took me back to his palace where his big brother was. Now he was good-looking. We sent the wedding invitations almost straight away.

Apparently when she found out she died of shock and grief. I mean I always knew she was a bit nutty - talking to a mirror and all - but that's no reason to drop down dead when you find out that your stepdaughter's found happiness at last.

As I said she had something against me but I don't know what.

Snow White.

Laura Burgess (10)
Sonning Common Primary School, Reading

Molly's Big Change!

Meet Molly, a rich, pretty girl. She couldn't ask for more. One day that all changed …

'What! I don't want to move to a farm. It's far too dirty.' Molly had just found out the most tragic thing had happened. Molly's dad had taken out a loan and couldn't pay it back. So, Molly had to work. She was used to, well, being clean.

The day had come! Molly's nightmare was just beginning.

When she unpacked she couldn't fit all of her things in her room. 'Could this get any worse?' Molly said to herself.

The next day she started work. She was in the pigsty. She had to look around when she dropped her bracelet. She bent down to pick it up when one of the pigs left a 'delivery'. 'Eeeewww!' Molly exclaimed. She dropped everything and ran into the house. Molly ran around like a maniac until she found her mum. When Molly's mum knew she realised Molly wasn't going to last long in this job.

For the next few days Molly had a horrid time. She was trampled on by cows, had fallen off a horse and was bitten by rats! She was fed up and decided to tell her mum she was not putting up with it. She had a talk with her mum and as it turned out no one in her family liked living on the farm. So she wasn't alone after all. Will she ever leave the farm?

Anna Snape
Wood's Foundation Primary School, Woodborough

James And The Beanstalk

One day in a village called Woodborough there was a boy named James who had nothing to do, when all of a sudden he saw a gigantic beanstalk in his backyard. So he decided to take a look at it. Then he had an idea, he would climb up it. When he reached the top he saw a castle, he decided to take a look. He knocked on the door and there in front of him was a 20 foot-giant with a name tag saying 'Joe'. So James said, 'Hello Joe.'

He replied, 'Hello James.'

James thought, *how does he know my name?*

Then he told James that he could grant him three wishes. So James said, 'I wish I could have all the money in the world,' so in front of James there was two tons of gold.

Joe said, 'Would you like to come in to finish your last two wishes?'

So James trotted inside and asked for a family car, and a big house. James was so excited and the giant helped James carry treasures to his new house. His family were grateful to the giant and they lived happily ever after.

George Gamble (10)
Wood's Foundation Primary School, Woodborough

The Giant Jacob And The Daisy

Once upon a time there lived a giant named Jacob. He was very poor and he didn't have any money. He lived in a city called London. Jacob and his mum were so poor that they lived in a gigantic hole. They only owned one horse.

Every day he made his mum do everything for him. He told his mum to go and sell the horse. She bumped into an old giant selling daisy seeds in his pockets. They did a trade, the horse for the daisy seeds, but these weren't ordinary seeds, these were special seeds. Jacob's mum went home and explained to Jacob what had happened.

He was furious and ripped the packet of daisy seeds in half in anger and chucked them out of the hole, and went to bed.

The next morning the big giant named Jacob saw a huge daisy. He couldn't believe his eyes. He rushed outside and started to climb the daisy. He saw a castle and he knocked on the door and a little boy answered the door. He was called Joe. Jacob started to bully Joe and be amazingly nasty.

The boy was getting really nervous and his knees started to knock together and he was so scared that he ran all the way to the daisy and climbed down. He looked up and said, 'You can't get me now!'

Joe cut the daisy down quickly.

Jacob Radford (10)
Wood's Foundation Primary School, Woodborough

Frankenstein And The Three Sloths

One day, three sloths were hanging around, when they saw the slowest monster of all, Frankenstein. The sloths ran away to lose him.

They needed a better house, so they used chocolate. They saw a parrot with a load of chocolate and paid him a pound. It took three hours building their house.

Frankenstein saw the chocolate. One sloth said, 'Go away from our chocolate.'

Frankenstein answered, 'I'm hungry,' and he ate it.

'Let's try medicine for the next house!'

The sloths saw a cat with medicine. One sloth said, 'How much?'

'Free, I hate it, take it,' Cat said. They froze the medicine and built their house.

Frankenstein had a tummy ache (it was all that chocolate). He found the frozen medicine. He ate loads. The sloths sneaked out. Before he saw them Frankenstein felt better with every bite. 'Let's try bricks.'

The sloths went to a human's house. Sloth One said, 'Hi, we are looking for some bricks.'

The man stroked Sloth One.

'We are stealing,' Sloth Two said.

They stole some bricks and built their house.

Frankenstein was better but still hungry. Frankenstein saw the Sloths' house, he had a bite. He said, 'My dead teeth can't eat this. Oh well, into the chimney and eat them.'

Frankenstein climbed into the chimney and the fire was on. He screamed, 'Why is my one weakness fire? Aaarrrgghhhh!'

Sloth One said, 'I smell chicken and steak.'

'You're right,' Sloth Two said.

They lived happily ever after.

David Walker (10)
Wood's Foundation Primary School, Woodborough

Wanted

At 2 o'clock in the morning the Big Bad Pig was found lying on the grass outside Cozudby station. The police forced him to tell them where his brother (The Big Bad Wolf) was. The Pig said, 'Alright! He is at Shebadia School.'

The police arrived and spotted the Big Bad Wolf lying on the ground, like a helpless child. Immediately he was taken into custody, along with his brother.

Now it is official, the two master criminals have been imprisoned! They have been imprisoned after 4 years on the run. The crimes they have committed are: pushing Humpty Dumpty off the wall, capturing Tinkerbell and holding at ransom all the king's horses and all the king's men.

Have you got any questions? Would you like more information? If so, log on to 'www.localnews.com/crimes' you can email us there.

Jack Boaden (Chief of Police).

Jack Boaden (10)
Wood's Foundation Primary School, Woodborough

Crisis At The Teddy Bears' Picnic

Once upon a time, at the teddy bears' picnic a terrible thing happened. The teddies were having a lovely time playing tag, but they didn't notice another teddy creep towards their picnic. He was muddy-brown whilst everyone else was golden-honey. He quietly opened the lunch basket and ...

'Oi, you come back here,' shouted Big Ted and ran after the bad teddy. The awful creature had stolen jam sandwiches. The teddies couldn't have their picnic without the jam sandwiches.

Toby bear put his paw on Edwina bear's shoulder. She was very sad, as she'd made the sandwiches. Ted was running after the teddy with the sandwiches. After an hour he returned with the bad teddy. Toby lifted the mask off his face, everybody gasped! It was their enemy Big Bad Bob Bear. 'Bob, what were you thinking?' squeaked Edwina.

'I wasn't invited to your picnic,' replied Bob. Ted, Toby and Edwina's face fell. They felt awful. Poor Bob.

'You can come, but do you promise never to steal again?' asked Toby.

'Of course,' agreed Bob.

So the teddies had their picnic.

Soon Bob changed his name to Big Brilliant Bob Bear. They were all friends and Bob got married to Edwina's sister Stella. They had a little baby called Milly Bear. They lived happily ever after and the story of the teddy bears' picnic lives on.

Eleanor Sharkey (10)
Wood's Foundation Primary School, Woodborough

Wanted Alive!

Reward - £10,000 each.

Wanted for fraud, witchcraft, highway robbery and breaking and entering. Every country in the world wants these partners-in-crime to get sent to jail. This person/animal is highly dangerous. Stay away at all costs. Altogether they have committed 291 different offences and crimes, if not found in a month, the reward will be raised to £20,000 each, and so on and so forth.

The wolf may be disguised as an old grandma or another wolf (he hasn't got the brightest of intellects). His voice will be rough and he might say 'blow your house down' a lot as well. He may be slightly scorched and smell smoky thanks to the Three Little Pigs who were given an OBE for their service, and did not want to reveal their location for security reasons.

The witch can change her appearance, so she could look like anyone. Do not let suspicious apple sellers into your house for it could be the witch. Her voice might be spooky and scary. She may laugh/ cackle quite often, so be on the look out for her or you'll probably get turned into a toad! She is extremely cunning, cruel and dangerous. If you see a gingerbread house *do not go in it*, or you'll be in mortal peril, instead phone 999 and ask for the police.

England will not rest until we find them.

From U.R. Nicked,

Head of Scotland Yard.

Ryan Skeels (10)
Wood's Foundation Primary School, Woodborough

Letter To The Agony Aunt

Dear Agony Aunt,

I need your help! I've found some trouble with three mice. I live on Eastwood Farm, in Epperstone. Mice have been intruding my property, please help!

Mice have been eating and nibbling at my furniture, but worst of all, at night when I'm trying to get to sleep, mice are nibbling my toes, and squeaking as loud as seventy-nine bulldozers! I had some ideas how to stop them:

1. I showed the mice a plastic piece of cheese but they're blind so that didn't work.
2. I put some cheese on a plate next to my bed at night with a hammer next to the plate, but I couldn't see the mice because it was too dark.
3. I tried threatening to chop their tails off with a carving knife, so I don't know what to do!

Please help me! Send a letter back to me if you have any other ideas; Eastwood Farm, Epperstone, NG14 ZB3.

Yours sincerely,

Farmers Wife aka Sarah.

Tamsin Smith (10)
Wood's Foundation Primary School, Woodborough

Patricia Pan

Once upon a time there was a hero called Patricia Pan and all the children adored her; 'I want to be Patricia now,' cried Wendy. Johnny, Susan and Wendy are brothers and sisters. Johnny is oldest at 13, Susan is second oldest at 7 years and Wendy is 16 months old.

'Well, I am Patricia Pan,' shouted somebody. The children turned around. It was *the* Patricia Pan, 'and you lot are coming to Level Land with me.'

They flew to Level Land. Well actually, the children held Patricia's hand and they finally arrived at Level Land. 'Where have my boys gone? They have run away and what about Tinkerbell, she was supposed to look after them. It is not like her to run away. Something is wrong!'

'Well have you got an enemy or something?' asked Susan, suspiciously.

'Well there is one, Captain Look!' said Patricia.

'There we go, where does he live?' said Johnny.

'Follow me, he is a pirate, but I know where his ship is,' shouted Patricia. They flew off and arrived on board his ship. Captain Look looked. They were just about to land when they heard *click, clock*. They knew when they heard that, Captain Look would fall off the ship and die. In fact, everyone knew.

That is exactly what happened. He fell off and got eaten by a shark. Tinkerbell and the boys came back from collecting food and they all lived in Level Land happily ever after.

Jane Fraser (9)
Wood's Foundation Primary School, Woodborough

The Ugly Duckling's Problem

Dear Sally (Agony Aunt),

I'm the Ugly Duckling. Nobody loves me, not even my mother! Everyone says I'm a disgrace, I look horrible. I have grey messy fur, my beak is an orange colour and it's lopsided. My quack sounds like a clunk, my eyes are too big and black and my feet are orange, fat and get in the way. I look terrible, but I always try my best to be friendly, kind and happy.

My problem is, no wants to be my friend. My mother doesn't want me, so when I'm frightened nobody's there for me to cuddle up to. I need another duckling like me, but I've searched the whole of Lake Town and there's nobody. When I go to the pond to eat bread the children give us, all the other ducks make sure I only get a few crumbs and the children are scared of me. Most of the day I'm crying. I really need a friend so I don't feel as bad. Is that possible?

Is there anyone the same as me in this world? When I grow up will I be beautiful? Will I ever have a friend? What will I do if no one ever likes me? What can I do to make me beautiful? Will my mother ever love me? What can I do? I'm very lonely. I hope you can find me a friend. Please, please, please help me.

Yours sincerely,

The Ugly Duckling.

Katherine Driver (10)
Wood's Foundation Primary School, Woodborough

Have You Seen The Big Bad Wolf?

Dear Chief of Police,

Please could you help us get rid of a disruptive wolf. Three little pigs called Dennis, Olivia and Jim have worked extremely hard to make some houses out of hay, straw and bricks. The wolf is being a real nuisance as he is continuously blowing down the house.

The pigs had a house each. First the wolf blew down Jim's house and tried to catch him but Jim was too fast and ran into Olivia's house. Next the wolf decided to blow down Olivia's house. He tried to eat both the pigs, but they were too fast and ran to Dennis' house. Finally the wolf blew Dennis' house down and tried to eat them all. They were all too fast and ran into the farm which had a 5-barred gate and an electric fence around it so the wolf couldn't get in.

Please could you help us catch the wolf. We are desperate. When you have caught him please, please could you lock him up forever! I hope you can help.

Thank you.
Yours sincerely,
Holly Smith
Local pig sanctuary owner.

Holly Smith (10)
Wood's Foundation Primary School, Woodborough

Watch Out For The Pudding!

Once upon a time there was a very pretty princess called Pamela. She had beautiful golden hair and brilliant blue eyes. She was very much respected by the citizens of Woodville (the village she ruled over) and was always fair to them.

One person however didn't respect Pamela. Granny Grump - her cruel grandmother - hated her. She was jealous of Pamela's good looks, as the old lady was frighteningly ugly, especially her warty, hooked nose.

One sunny day, Pamela came home to her palace after a walk through the woods and found a hot blackberry pudding on her table. She was surprised. Who could've put it there? It smelled delicious. She couldn't resist, and ate a spoonful. It was scrumptious.

Meanwhile, Granny Grump was watching through the window and cackled menacingly. Pamela had fallen into the trap!

Next morning Pamela woke up to find her face covered in purple spots. 'It must have been the blackberry pudding!' she shrieked. Now she knew who had put the pudding there, and they would pay!

In court the next day, Granny Grump was severely told off by the judge for tricking innocent Pamela (a fabulous ruler) and sent to prison!

Granny Grump was seething. How dare she be put in prison! After all, she'd only played rotten tricks, robbed a few houses and teased important people!

Everybody was delighted Granny Grump was in prison. It served her right. Pamela discovered some spot cream in Boots, and everyone lived happily ever after - except perhaps Granny Grump!

Josie Perry (9)
Wood's Foundation Primary School, Woodborough

Joe And The Beanstalk

One morning Joe woke up and noticed a giant beanstalk in his garden! The beanstalk was nearly as big as his garden! He decided to take further action by climbing up the enormous beanstalk.

Eventually he got to the top after half an hour climbing. Amazingly there was a massive castle in front of him. The door was wide open so he went in. To his surprise there was a giant monster in front of him. He tried to run away but the door shut! It had 3 eyes, 10 legs and orange skin!

'It's all right, I won't hurt you,' the monster said in a friendly voice. Meanwhile however he had two horrible children who wanted to eat Joe! The following day they were just about to eat Joe when he slid down the beanstalk and chopped it down! Joe lived happily ever after.

Joe Desmond (10)
Wood's Foundation Primary School, Woodborough

Lumpey Dumpey The Silly Egg

Once upon a time an egg called Lumpey Dumpey wanted to climb a mountain and conquer it for egg rights. When he got up to the top he sat on his rucksack that had wheels, he slid all the way back down leaving half of the flag in his hand and the other still on the mountain.

Smash!

There was egg everywhere but when the police got to the scene the murderer had gone.

If you catch the rucksack monster please contact police officer Wallop immediately.

Thank you.

(Phone 999.)

Jemma Lynch (10)
Wood's Foundation Primary School, Woodborough

The Two Triplets And The Odd One Out!

'Blahdy, blahdy. blah!' Frogney cried, he stuffed his fingers in his ears and started singing out loud. He had been in a massive strop all morning and his family were fed up.

'You're getting older now, Frogalina and Froger, you are going to have to leave my house and buy one of your own!' the triplets' mum shouted over Frogney's cries.

'Where will we go?' Froger asked. 'Will we be separated?'

'No, you two will stay together but Frogney will live on his own.' The two children gasped.

Let me tell you a bit about the triplets, well, you might have guessed what Frogney's like. He's mean, cruel and hates sleeping. Frogalina loves dancing but hates football and Froger loves sleeping but hates, hates, hates Monday mornings!

Froger and Frogalina were all packed and ready for a house of their own, but Frogney had only packed a pair of socks!

'Are you packed Frogney? You're leaving!' their mum shouted.

'No!' Frogney answered. 'Help me!'

'No!' Mum cried. An hour later Frogney was walking around, trying to find a house for himself, while Froger and Frogalina had moved into a lovely cottage and were already unpacking their things. he soon came to an old house, he walked inside. He was really scared so he called his old house. His mum let him stay with his siblings and after a while he soon moved in forever, and they lived happily ever after!

Elicia Cowley (10)
Wood's Foundation Primary School, Woodborough

Tiger Legs

In a small town called Woodborough, lived a young girl called Emily who lived with her dad, Tom, an inventor and not forgetting Emily's adopted tiger cub, Stripes. He was a fluffy bundle of fun but his life was dull because the circus had thrown him out. Luckily Emily was there to help.

At noon Dad invited Emily to see his new invention, (Emily was unsure as last time she slipped on to a screwdriver and pushed down a button, now Emily and Stripes can mind read each other) she decided to go but only if Stripes came.

As Dad slowly opened the enormous metal door down to the laboratory Emily was having second thoughts but yet she forced herself down. Wow! Her father's invention was fantastic, the machine was a leg transplanter. It was just a shame that Stripes had to ruin it by falling on the marvellously white sheet and pushing down one of the buttons and suddenly, *whizz, bang, wallop!* The leg transplanter picked up the closest two things and changed their legs around.

Oh no! What has happened! It couldn't be happening! Stripes and Emily had swapped legs around. Luckily for them Dad had invented a time machine to swap legs back! (Phew!)

All the lights were out apart from the 'I don't like my legs machine'. That was buzzing away happily to itself.

In the end Emily and Stripes got their own legs back. Emily, Dad and Stripes lived happily ever after.

Rachel Martin (10)
Wood's Foundation Primary School, Woodborough

The Three Little Puppies And The Big Bad Bird

Long, long ago there lived three little puppies. One called Joe, one called Jay and one called John. One day they were being naughty so their Mum sent them outside, so they built a house themselves to live in. John went to the paper shop to buy a paper to build his house.

Jay went to his favourite place the sweet shop. He made his house out of sweets. Chocolate here, sugar there.

Joe was the cleverest he built his house out of wood. He found the wood in a forest.

All of a sudden there was a big shadow on the ground and the Big Bad Bird came to John's house and said, 'Give me a giant worm I will flap your house down.'

John shouted, 'No!'

So Big Bad Bird flapped and his house fell down.

Then Big Bad Bird went to Jay's house and said the same again as he did to John and Jay said, 'No!' and then the Big Bad Bird flapped and flapped and his house fell down. Then the Big Bad Bird went to Joe's house and Joe had a plan, as John phoned him. Joe went to get a trap and then brought it home.

The Big Bad Bird flew into the trap and he was gone forever. They lived happily ever after.

Eve McElhone (10)
Wood's Foundation Primary School, Woodborough

Little Pink Riding Hood

One bright sunny day a little girl called Little Pink Riding Hood was skipping in the garden when her mum asked her to take a pie to Grandad. So she hopped off.

On the way to Grandad's house she forgot her cloak so she ran all the way home. When she got home she got her furry pink cloak and began to walk again.

Grandad went looking for Little Pink Riding Hood. When she got to Grandad's house, suddenly a wolf appeared and gobbled her up. 'Yum-yum,' he whispered. He jumped into the bed, grabbed a pie and a drink, and began. Grandad looked everywhere but he couldn't find Pink Riding Hood. So he went, gave up and went home. When he got there the wolf was fast asleep. Grandad got a pan and banged the wolf on the head who melted into sand. Suddenly Little Pink Riding Hood appeared out of thin air. Grandad picked up Little Pink Riding Hood and hugged her.

'I love you,' cried Little Pink Riding Hood.

'I love you too,' cried Grandad. So they walked to Little Pink Riding Hood's house and had pie! Yum-yum!

Patrick McCrossen (10)
Wood's Foundation Primary School, Woodborough

A Winnie The Pooh Adventure

Once upon a time in Hundred Acre Wood it was Pooh and Tigger's birthday. Tigger's invitations were beautiful, they had sparkly sequins and a lovely picture of Tigger on them.

They read:

'To ...

Please come to my party, at my house.

1pm to 6pm.

Love from Tigger.

P.S. Bring some food, drinks and games.

I hope you like chocolate cake!'

While Tigger was handing out his invitations, Pooh was making his invitations, which had the same words but with a picture of him.

Both parties were on the same day at the same time.

'What are you doing?' said Tigger.

'Handing out my invitations,' said Pooh.

'I am, they will all come to mine,' said Tigger.

Pooh stormed off.

The day came and it was 3pm, and there was no one at either of the parties. As time passed Tigger thought Pooh had ripped up his invites. 'I'm disgusted,' said Tigger, as he stormed out the door.

Knock, knock.

'You stole all my party guests,' said Tigger.

'But they're not here, look,' said Pooh.

'They're all hiding,' said Tigger.

'No they're not,' said Pooh.

'Sorry,' said Tigger.

'Let's go and see what's going on,' said Pooh.

Knock, knock.

'Hello,' said Owl.

'What are you doing? Why aren't you at my party?' said Tigger.

'No one came because they didn't want to upset either of you,' said Owl.

'Surprise!' shouted everyone.

So they had a joint party for both Pooh and Tigger.

Elvey Craig-Dennis (10)
Wood's Foundation Primary School, Woodborough

Have You Seen The Three Little Wolves?

They have been missing for over 2 days, and they're only 10 years old. Their favourite places are: the train station, sweet shop, cinema and Pizza Hut. Their names are: Kojo, Todo and Nomo.

What happened?

They were building their houses but when they'd finished and had gone inside their houses, the big bad pig came along and tried to blow down Kojo's house which was made of straw.

They went to Todo's house, which was made out of hay, but the pig followed them on to Nomo's house and blew that down as well.

So the three little wolves ran away.

If you can find or have seen the three little wolves then please contact me on 19625018423.

Yours sincerely,

Emma Rosenberg.

Emma Rosenberg (10)
Wood's Foundation Primary School, Woodborough

The Fairy Times

There was a tailor and his wife who made clothes for a number of years, but the tailor was actually very lazy. His wife, Mrs Tailor, does all the work.

Two days ago she fell asleep at night. After her husband had gone to bed. Lazy bones! Silently, two pixies crept into the sewing room. They saw the material laid out for sewing. They saw how tired Mrs Tailor looked, and the pixies set to work sewing the pieces of material together. When Mrs Tailor woke up she saw, to her amazement, the material had been sewn together leaving some perfect clothes. The same thing happened three nights in a row. On the fourth night she kept her eyes a bit open so she could see what was going on. She saw the pixies come and climb up the table leg and start sewing. At dawn the pixies packed up and left.

Mrs Tailor was very pleased with what the pixies had done for her, so she decided to make some clothes for them. First she made a dress for each of them, one was blue and one was red. Then she made a coat for each of them, a blue coat and a red coat. She also cooked some cakes for them.

That night she left the clothes on the table and stood behind a curtain. The pixies came in and saw the clothes. They were delighted. Mrs Tailor felt very pleased, as she watched them dance about.

Chloë Roper (10)
Wood's Foundation Primary School, Woodborough

The Three Little Sheep

Sid, Sam and Shaun were 3 sheep who lived with their mother. One day the mother told them to go and make their own houses. So off they went to find materials to build their new homes.

Sid asked a horse for some bricks and the horse gave him some. Sam asked a farmer for some metal and the farmer gave him some. Shaun asked her dog for some titanium and the dog gave him some.

They all built their houses. One day a big bad bull came along and asked if he could come in. Sid replied, 'No!'

'I will ram your house down,' shouted Benny, the bull. That's what he did. The house fell down and Sid ran to Sam's house.

Benny went to Sam's house and asked if he could come in. Sam replied, 'No!' The bull rammed this down and Sam and Sid ran to Shaun's house.

Benny went to Shaun's house and asked if he could come in.

Shaun replied, 'No!' Benny rammed the house but he got knocked out. Their mum moved in with the sheep and they lived happily ever after. Benny learned never to be mean again. He ended up in hospital with a horn broken off!

Adam Clarke (10)
Wood's Foundation Primary School, Woodborough